GOLD
experience
2ND EDITION

WORKBOOK

A2

Key for
Schools

CONTENTS

Listening	Speaking	Writing	Review
listen to someone talking about their family; classroom language; spelling	talking about your family; classroom language		
topic: art club **task:** gap-fill	**topic:** free time **task:** asking and answering questions about free time	**topic:** clubs **task:** an email	unit check 1 review: starter–unit 1 (p15)
topic: technology **task:** multiple choice (pictures)	**topic:** a birthday party **task:** describing photos	**topic:** apps and gadgets **task:** a paragraph	unit check 2 review: units 1–2 (p23)
topic: schools around the world **task:** multiple choice	**topic:** school **task:** talking about school	**topic:** a school trip **task:** a description	unit check 3 review: units 1–3 (p31)
topic: lost in a shopping centre **task:** multiple choice	**topic:** services in town **task:** asking and answering questions	**topic:** my favourite place in town **task:** a review	unit check 4 review: units 1–4 (p39)
topic: entertainment **task:** multiple choice (pictures)	**topic:** entertainment **task:** discussion	**topic:** personal anecdotes **task:** a story	unit check 5 review: units 1–5 (p47)
topic: what makes holidays fun? **task:** matching	**topic:** holiday plans **task:** talking about holiday activities	**topic:** school and family trips **task:** an email	unit check 6 review: units 1–6 (p55)
topic: sport **task:** multiple choice (pictures)	**topic:** sport **task:** asking and answering questions	**topic:** sport **task:** an email about a new sport	unit check 7 review: units 1–7 (p63)
topic: I've seen a bear! **task:** three-option multiple choice	**topic:** outdoor activities **task:** discussion	**topic:** travel **task:** a postcard	unit check 8 review: units 1–8 (p71)
topic: fun food **task:** gap-fill	**topic:** hobbies and free time activities **task:** discussion	**topic:** a day at home **task:** a story	unit check 9 review: units 1–9 (p79)

Starter This is me!

1 Complete Joe's family tree with these words.

aunty brother cousin dad grandma grandpa ~~mum~~ sister uncle

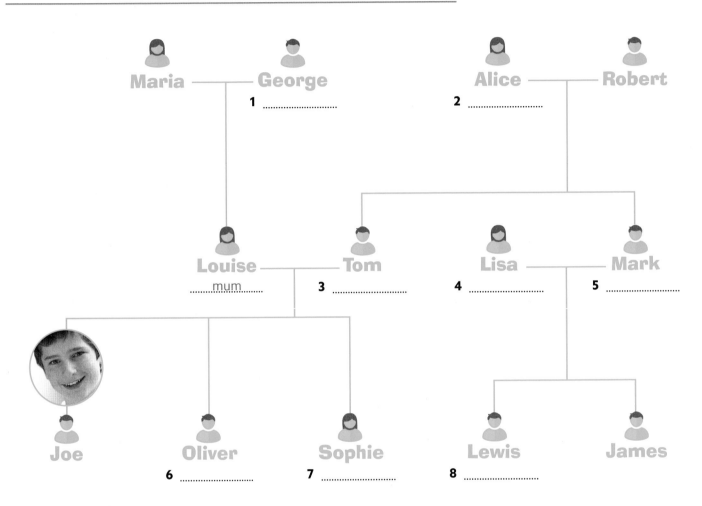

Maria — George
1 ....

Alice — Robert
2 ....

Louise — Tom
......mum......   3 ....

Lisa — Mark
4 ....   5 ....

Joe   Oliver   Sophie
6 ....   7 ....

Lewis   James
8 ....

2 Complete the sentences about Joe's family.

Louise is Joe's ......mum...... .

1 Sophie is Oliver's ....
2 Lisa is Lewis and James' ....
3 Maria is Sophie's ....
4 Mark is Oliver's ....
5 Louise is James' ....
6 Oliver is Lewis' ....
7 Alice and Robert are Lewis and James' ....

3 🔊 S.1 Listen to Joe talking about four people in his family. Write the name of each person he is talking about.

1 ....
2 ....
3 ....
4 ....

4 Look at the information and find these things. More than one answer may be possible.

a surname ___Milton___

1 a street name _____

2 a website address _____

3 a postcode _____

4 a nationality _____

5 a first name _____

6 a date _____

7 a telephone number _____

imetable

to Saturdays
ic holidays

0945 1045 1145 1245 1345 1445 1545 1645
0950 1050 1150 1250 1345 1450 1550 1650
0955
1045 11
1050 11
1 1111 1
50
0950
55
0955
350 0950

Sundays
public holidays

1055 1355 1455 1545 1655
1055 1355 1255 1845 1855
1250 1350 1450
545 1645 1745
550 1650 1750
611 1711 1811
545 1645 1745

1811
1655
1655

A Toronto City Bus Pass

11–16-year-olds

Name:	Rosanna Milton
Valid until:	12 October
Bus pass no.:	88955679

B GLOBALSPORT

Name: Agata Jaworski

Age: 12

Member: tennis club

Global Sports, Eastgate Street, Bristol, BS1 2WH
Tel: 0117 443 5788

C Pet Passport

Name:	Rocky
Nationality:	Irish
Owner:	Lewis Stephens
I.D. number:	6785J45426

D www.friends-page.org.uk   Close X

Noah Williams

INFORMATION

Born on:	25 June
Studies at:	Greenville High School
Likes:	Manchester United

FAMILY

Ethan Williams (brother)   View all

Isabella Williams (sister)

E Middleton Language School

First name: Alejandro
Last name: Garcia
Nationality: Spanish
Age: 13
Expiry date: 23 March

Middleton Language School | Main Square
Oxford OX2 6YE | Tel: 0186 767 534
www.middleton-lang.ac.uk

5 Look at the information and answer the questions.

Who's got a brother?
Noah Williams

1 Who goes to a school in Oxford?

....

2 What nationality is Rocky?

....

3 What sport does Agata play?

....

4 Where does Rosanna Milton live?

....

5 Whose birthday is in June?

....

6 Who likes football?

....

1 **Choose the correct words to complete the sentences.**

(Put) / Get your hand up when you know the correct answer.

1 **Do** / **Match** the words with the photos of different kinds of food.

2 Open your books and **turn** / **move** to page twenty-four.

3 **Write** / **Complete** the text with one word for each space.

4 Work in **pairs** / **partners** and answer questions one to ten.

5 **Write** / **Complete** your name at the top of your piece of paper.

2 🔊 S.2 **Complete the conversation with these words/phrases. Listen and check your answers.**

---

can   here you are   match   ~~put your hand up~~
repeat   turn to   work in pairs

A: Morning, everyone. What's the date today? <u>Put your hand up</u> , please! Yes, Adam.

B: It's Monday the tenth of March.

A: Thank you, Adam. OK, can everyone **¹**..................................... page sixty-three, please?

C: Sorry, can you **²**..................................... that, please?

A: Page sixty-three. Now, I want you to **³**..................................... and do Exercise 1. You **⁴**..................................... the words with the pictures.

D: Mrs Stock, **⁵**..................................... I have a pencil, please?

A: Yes, **⁶**..................................... .

3 **Choose the correct answer, A, B or C.**

What's 'Jeudi' in English?

A That's French.

(B) Look it up in the dictionary.

C You're correct, 'Jeudi' isn't English.

1 Can you repeat the last question, please?

A Yes, of course.

B Yes, you're welcome.

C Yes, here you are.

2 Can I have some paper, please?

A Yes, I have some paper.

B Yes, here you are.

C Yes, I can.

3 What does 'pleasant' mean?

A It is an adjective.

B Yes, it does.

C It means 'nice'.

4 What page is the exercise on?

A It's there.

B Yes, it is.

C Page 45.

5 Can I go to the toilet, please?

A Yes, in a minute.

B Yes, that's right.

C Yes, thank you.

4 Match the words (1–7) with the things in the picture (A–H).

poster _C_

2 cupboard _____

4 chair _____

6 bookcase _____

1 clock _____

3 bin _____

5 computer _____

7 noticeboard _____

5 Complete the text with *there is* or *there are*.

This is my classroom at school. _There is_ a cupboard and **1**_____ a bookcase. **2**_____ lots of books in the bookcase. **3**_____ a noticeboard on the wall and **4**_____ two posters on the wall. **5**_____ lots of chairs.

6 Complete the sentences with *a, an, some* or *any*.

There is _____a_____ clock.

1 There aren't _____ students.

2 There isn't _____ bag.

3 There are _____ chairs.

4 There aren't _____ shelves.

5 There isn't _____ apple.

6 There's _____ poster.

7 There are _____ books in the bookcase.

7 🔊 S.3 Listen and complete the conversation.

A: How do you **1**_____ bookcase?

B: It's B- **2**_____ O-K-C-A-S-E.

A: Sorry, can you say that **3**_____ , please?

B: Yes, **4**_____ .

8 🔊 S.4 Listen and answer the questions. Write the words.

1 _____   **6** _____

2 _____   **7** _____

3 _____   **8** _____

4 _____   **9** _____

5 _____   **10** _____

9 🔊 S.5 Listen again and check your answers.

READING

1 Complete the sentences with these words.

| artist bats career competition gamer prize |

1 My friend is an amazing .... She likes drawing people.

2 The winners get a .... of £50.

3 Jake wants a .... in food. He wants a job as a chef.

4 I really want to win the school singing .... this year.

5 Lots of .... fly round our house at night.

6 Isobel is a brilliant .... She plays video games all the time.

2 Read the article and match the people (1–3) with the photos (A–C).

3 e Read the article again. For each question, choose the correct answer.

	Patrick	Tomas	Emilia
1 Which person does their hobby every day?	A	B	C
2 Which person wants to be in a competition on TV?	A	B	C
3 Which person does their hobby with a family member?	A	B	C
4 Which person reads about their hobby?	A	B	C
5 Which person wants to earn money from their hobby in the future?	A	B	C
6 Which person lives in a house?	A	B	C
7 Which person likes doing art?	A	B	C

FREE TIME! How do you spend yours?

1 Patrick Summers is from Edinburgh and his hobby's fishing. He goes fishing with his friends. His parents don't fish, but they always watch Patrick in fishing competitions. Patrick goes fishing every day in the summer. He goes to the river near his house. He can see the river from his bedroom – he lives on the third floor. Patrick likes learning about fishing from magazines. He also enjoys painting pictures of fish.

2 Tomas Kowlaski is from Manchester and loves baking. He's the only person in his family who enjoys it. He makes all the cakes and biscuits at home. The family flat often smells of his baking! He also helps his mum cook dinner nearly every day, but on Saturdays they usually buy pizza. One day Tomas wants to have his own cake shop or bakery. He also wants to be on a TV show like 'Junior Masterchef'. He loves watching the competition with his sister.

3 Emilia Stevenson is from London and loves singing. She's in a band with two school friends and her cousin. Singing is the first thing she does every morning. Her favourite place to sing is her garden. Emilia watches the TV singing competition 'The Voice' every Saturday. She loves the show, but doesn't like singing in competitions herself. In her free time, Emilia also likes reading books by Philip Pullman. She loves the drawings in his books.

GRAMMAR

present simple, adverbs of frequency

1 Choose the correct words to complete the sentences.

1 They **doesn't / don't** like fishing.
2 Emily **take / takes** amazing photographs.
3 He **don't / doesn't** go camping.
4 The children **play / plays** video games after school.
5 Sam and Oli **goes / go** to the cinema every month.
6 **Does / Do** they watch TV on Saturday mornings?

2 Complete the email with the present simple form of the verbs in brackets.

Hi Juliette,

This year's summer camp ¹.................... (be) brilliant! We ².................... (do) lots of different activities here. In the morning we do activities outside. Sometimes I ³.................... (play) football and sometimes I go fishing. In the afternoon we do art and music. I ⁴.................... (enjoy) painting and drawing. My brother ⁵.................... (like) the music classes here. He ⁶.................... (love) playing the guitar. In the evenings we often ⁷.................... (watch) a film together or play video games. It ⁸.................... (be) great fun!

See you soon,
Freddy

3 🔊 1.1 Complete the questions with the present simple form of the verbs in brackets. Listen and check your answers.

....Do.... your parents ....enjoy.... (enjoy) playing board games?
1 .... your dad .... (listen) to music?
2 .... you .... (have) a favourite hobby?
3 .... your best friend .... (go) to a drawing class on Wednesdays?
4 .... you .... (collect) anything?
5 .... your cousins .... (watch) a lot of TV?

4 Write short answers for the questions in Ex 3.

....Yes, they do.................................... ✓
1 .... ✗
2 .... ✓
3 .... ✗
4 .... ✓
5 .... ✗

5 Put these words in the correct place.

~~always~~   never   not often   not usually   often   sometimes

.........always......... **100%**
1 ....
2 ....
3 ....
4 ....
5 ....   **0%**

6 Put the words in the correct order to make sentences.

TV / usually / in the evening / my parents / watch
My parents usually watch TV in the evening.
1 always / my singing lessons / fun / are
....
2 in June / there / sometimes / is / a chess competition
....
3 Kiera / never / her music lessons / enjoys
....
4 go / often / in / the / holidays / shopping / we
....

VOCABULARY

free time

1 Match the photos (1–8) with these hobbies.

---

baking   camping   dancing   drawing   fishing   painting
reading   singing

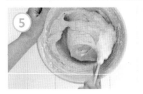

2 🔊 1.2 Complete the questions with one word in each gap. Listen and check your answers.

1 A: Do you like .... ?
   B: Yes, I have my own tent.

2 A: Do you .... cakes at home?
   B: No, but I like making bread.

3 A: Do your brother and sister .... ?
   B: My sister does. She has a nice voice, but my brother doesn't.

4 A: Do you always .... a book or comic before you go to bed?
   B: Yes, every night.

5 A: Does Alice enjoy .... ?
   B: Yes, she does ballet.

6 A: Do you do .... in your art class?
   B: Yes, we do. And we do drawing, too.

3 Read the blog post. Choose the correct answer for each gap.

What am I into?
Lots of things!

It's difficult to choose my favourite hobby or interest. I <u>have</u> lots of different interests. I love **1**....... my guitar and singing. I like **2**....... to music with my friends. Sometimes we meet at my house and we watch YouTube videos. We also watch **3**....... together. I enjoy playing football after school. I love everything about football. My friends and I collect football cards. My favourite player is Lionel Messi. My friend Jack **4**....... postcards. He has about 350! My sister is seventeen years old. She likes going **5**....... at the weekend. She often goes to the cinema with her friends. Her hobby is **6**....... . She loves making cakes – and I love eating her cakes!

	A make	**B** take	**C** have
1	**A** listening	**B** playing	**C** singing
2	**A** listening	**B** watching	**C** playing
3	**A** comics	**B** cartoons	**C** cards
4	**A** collects	**B** watches	**C** plays
5	**A** sleepovers	**B** shopping	**C** drawing
6	**A** eating	**B** making	**C** baking

Extend

4 Choose the correct words to complete the phrases.

1 do / make / play a board game
2 go / do / collect model planes
3 collect / play / listen the keyboard
4 read / do / watch magazines
5 do / make / take photographs
6 play / read / go chess

5 Complete the sentences with words from Ex 4.

1 My cousins .... model planes.
2 I always .... photographs on holiday.
3 My brother often .... chess with my grandad.
4 She plays the .... in a band.
5 Luke doesn't .... magazines.
6 Our family sometimes plays a .... on Sundays.

LISTENING

1 🔊 1.3 **Listen to a phone message. Why does Matt leave Jacob the message?**

A to tell Jacob about his new hobby

B to give Jacob some information

C to ask about dance lessons

2 ℮ 🔊 1.4 **Listen again. For each question, write the correct answer. Write one word or a number or a date or a time.**

☐ ☐ ☐ ☐ ☐ ☐ ☐ ☐ ☐ ☐ ☐

Dance classes

Day: .....Tuesday.....

Start time: ¹............................ p.m.

Price per lesson: £²............................

Address of dance school: 68 ³............................
Street

Teacher's surname: ⁴............................

Dance school phone number: ⁵............................

Bring: ⁶............................

3 🔊 1.5 **Listen again. Are the sentences true (T) or false (F)?**

1 The street dancing classes start next week. ....

2 The classes end at a quarter to six. ....

3 You can pay for a group of eight lessons or pay each week. ....

4 The school is in the middle of town. ....

5 The school's door is green. ....

6 Matt says Jacob can see the teacher dance on YouTube. ....

much/many

4 **Complete the table with these words.**

~~bread~~ cakes friends fun hobbies money music people
time video games

much	many
bread	

5 **Complete the conversations with *much* or *many*.**

1 A: How .... musical instruments do you play?

B: Two – the piano and the violin.

2 A: Have you got .... music on your phone?

B: Yeah, I've got about 300 songs on it.

3 A: How .... people go to the chess club?

B: About twelve.

4 A: Do you have .... free time?

B: Not after school, but I do at weekends.

5 A: I want a new hobby, but I don't have .... money.

B: My hobby's singing. It doesn't cost any money.

6 **Complete the email. Write one word for each gap.**

Hi Poppy,

Do you want to come to art club ......with...... me? There aren't ¹............................ people in the club. There ²............................ about six people and they're all really nice. It doesn't cost ³............................ money. It's only £2 a week. We do a lot of drawing and some painting, but we don't do ⁴............................ painting. It starts at 4 p.m. and it's ⁵............................ Wednesdays.

I hope ⁶............................ can come!

Harry

SPEAKING

1 Choose the correct words to complete the sentences.

1 What hobbies **do you have / does you have / have you**?

2 **What / Who / When** do you go to chess club?

3 **Is Lara / Lara do / Does Lara** good at dancing?

4 **Where play / Do you play / You play** table tennis?

5 Does your sister **enjoying / enjoy / enjoys** singing?

6 Where **does you like / do you likes / do you like** to read?

2 Read the questions. Choose the correct answer, A, B or C.

1 Do you like dancing?

  A Not really. I think it's brilliant.

  B Yes, but I'm not very good at it.

  C Yes, I hate it!

2 Is Marilena good at painting?

  A Yes, she does.

  B Yes, she's brilliant!

  C Yes, she paints.

3 When do you like listening to music?

  A In the evenings.

  B Sometimes.

  C Rock and pop music.

4 Do you like going to the cinema?

  A Yes, I like the weekends.

  B Yes, I like my friends.

  C Yes, I like sci-fi films.

5 How often do you go shopping?

  A Every Saturday morning.

  B With my best friend.

  C I usually buy clothes and shoes.

6 Do you collect anything?

  A I go to chess club.

  B Fishing and football.

  C Baseball caps. I've got eighty-six.

7 What are you good at?

  A Yes, I'm very good.

  B I hate dancing.

  C I think I'm good at drawing.

8 When do you and your friends usually play video games?

  A At weekends.

  B No, we don't.

  C We love video games.

3 Put the words in the correct order to make questions.

1 do / how / spend / time / on your / you / much / hobby?

....

2 to / many / you / go / how / clubs / do?

....

3 much / on your hobbies / you / how / do / spend?

....

4 have / how / hobbies / you / many / do?

....

5 much / watch / TV / do / how / you?

....

6 prizes / have / do / you / many / how?

....

4 Answer the questions in Ex 3.

1 ....

2 ....

3 ....

4 ....

5 ....

6 ....

5 Complete the sentences to make them true for you.

1 I enjoy ....

2 I love ....

3 I hate ....

4 I'm brilliant at ....

5 I'm not very good at ....

WRITING

Chess club

- Every Tuesday in the library
- 3.30–5.00 p.m.
- No food or drinks!
- It's free. 😊

1 Read the information and answer the questions.

1 Where is the chess club?

2 What time does the chess club start?

3 Can you bring sandwiches?

4 Do you have to pay?

2 Complete the conversation with these words.

> join   learn   meet   starts   time   welcome

A: I love the new dance club. It's great! We
¹ .... every Friday after school at Groove
Dance Studio.

B: Cool! What ² .... does it start?

A: It ³ .... at 7.15 p.m. We ⁴ .... a new
dance every week.

B: Can I ⁵ .... ?

A: Yes! Beginners are ⁶ ....

3 Put the words in the correct order to make sentences.

1 you / to guitar club / with me / to go / do / want?

....

2 every / after school / Thursday / it's

....

3 in / it's / 2B / room

....

4 starts / it / at 4.15 / at 5.00 / and / finishes

....

5 good / it's / fun

....

6 do / you / think / what?

....

4 Put the correct punctuation in the e-mail.

hi dan

do you want to go to chess club with me it's on
tuesdays after school we meet in the library at 3.30
we play for about an hour and a half it's really good
fun what do you think

chris

5 Complete the email with these words.

> do   hi   library   starts   take   want

¹ .... Elizabeth,

Do you ² .... to go to the photography
club? It ³ .... tomorrow after school.
We meet in the ⁴ .... at 4 p.m. We go to
different places to ⁵ .... photos. It's really
good. What ⁶ .... you think?

Megan

6 e Write an email to a friend. Invite him/her to your
table tennis club. Tell him/her the time, day and place
the club meets. Remember to start and finish in a
friendly way. Write 25 words or more.

UNIT CHECK

1 Match the questions (1–6) with the answers (A–F).

1 Do you go shopping with your parents? ....
2 Does your sister go to a chess club? ....
3 Do Ben and Karen like painting at school? ....
4 Do they go to the cinema? ....
5 Does Matthew collect anything? ....
6 Does Jane play the piano? ....

A Yes, she does. She goes to a club at school.
B Yes, they love films.
C Yes, he does. He's got 600 stamps.
D Yes, I do. We go every Saturday.
E No, she doesn't. She doesn't like music.
F No, they don't. They only like drawing.

2 Complete the questions with *much* or *many*.

1 How .... video games do you own?
2 How .... free time have you got?
3 How .... shopping do you do online?
4 How .... books do you read in a year?
5 How .... money do you spend on your hobbies?
6 How .... people collect football cards in your class?

3 Choose the correct words to complete the sentences.

1 Joe's not very good at **paint / painting**.
2 Emily goes **fishes / fishing** with her dad and brother every Sunday.
3 David and Cathy **play / playing** in a rock band.
4 We usually **draw / drawing** objects or people in our art class.
5 They enjoy **read / reading** comics.
6 Do you like **sing / singing**?

4 Complete the text with the present simple form of these verbs.

go   love   meet   not like   play   watch

At the weekend Matt **1** .... shopping with his mum and sister. He **2** .... shopping. He thinks it's boring. In the afternoon he **3** .... his friends in the park. In the summer they **4** .... football. In the evening Matt **5** .... a film. He **6** .... films!

5 Look at the information about Leo and Fiona. Write sentences using the prompts.

	Leo	Fiona
play video games after school	often	not usually
go on a sleepover at the weekend	never	sometimes
watch YouTube videos with friends	not often	often
listen to the radio in the morning	not usually	always

Leo / play video games after school
Leo often plays video games after school.

1 Fiona / play video games after school
....

2 Leo / go on a sleepover at the weekend
....

3 Fiona / go on a sleepover at the weekend
....

4 Leo / watch YouTube videos with friends
....

5 Fiona / watch YouTube videos with friends
....

6 Leo / listen to the radio in the morning
....

7 Fiona / listen to the radio in the morning
....

REVIEW: STARTER–UNIT 1

1 Complete the sentences with *there is* or *there are*.

1 .... a chess club at my school.
2 .... three dance classes on Saturday mornings.
3 .... an important fishing competition this weekend.
4 .... lots of people in my camera club.
5 .... more information about the clubs on the school website.
6 .... a good film at the cinema at the moment.
7 .... twelve students in my dance class.
8 .... time for a snack before class. Come on, I'm hungry!

2 Choose the correct words to complete the sentences.

1 He never **win / wins** prizes in competitions.
2 **Do / Does** your sister like fishing?
3 Emma and Lucy **don't / doesn't** play the guitar.
4 There **isn't / aren't** any chocolate in the cupboard.
5 What does 'exhausted' **mean / means**?
6 I have **some / a** new pair of trainers.
7 I **don't usually / usually don't** play tennis on Mondays.
8 There aren't **much / many** good videos on that website.

3 Match 1–6 with A–F to make sentences.

1 My uncle Tom is   A postcards from different places.
2 You need a passport to   B GL7 3RT.
3 My little sister collects   C to Martha's party.
4 She has an invitation   D my mum's brother.
5 Our postcode is   E repeat the question, please?
6 Sorry, can you   F leave the country.

4 Complete the sentences. Write one word for each gap.

1 Alex has .... really interesting hobby.
2 Table tennis club is .... Thursday afternoons.
3 Dance class starts .... 4.45 p.m.
4 I don't have .... free time after school. Only an hour.
5 You don't need to wear .... special clothes to the club.
6 The music school .... not far from here.
7 .... your brother collect model planes?
8 What time do you usually .... to bed on Saturdays?

5 ⓔ Read the text. Choose the correct answer for each gap.

How to find the right activity for you

What do you .do. in your free time? Maybe you watch films or **¹**....... to music. It's always fun to find a new interest. It **²**....... also a good way to make friends and learn new things. How do you find the right activity or interest for you? You need to ask yourself some questions. For example, do you like spending time outside or inside? A great hobby to do outside is **³**....... or fishing. Do you enjoy being on your own or with other people? There are lots of clubs that do sport. There are also clubs for making things. Painting, **⁴**....... and baking clubs are popular examples of these kinds of clubs. The important thing is to try something new. And **⁵**....... yourself!

	A make	Ⓑ do	C go
1	A listen	B hear	C play
2	A has	B is	C makes
3	A collecting	B baking	C camping
4	A reading	B singing	C drawing
5	A enjoy	B please	C prefer

15

2 Are you online?

READING

1 Choose the correct words to complete the sentences.

1 My friend is a **vlogger** / **vlog**. She makes weekly cooking videos.

2 I'm a **member** / **relation** of our school computer club.

3 There's an interesting **story** / **report** in the newspaper about the future of computers.

4 This is my favourite online **translator** / **vlog**. It's about fashion.

5 Our science **project** / **teacher** this month is about space.

6 My brother is twenty and goes to **high school** / **university** in London.

2 Look at the pictures in the report. What do you think it is about? Read it quickly and check your answers.

3 Read the report again and answer the questions.

1 How many days is Marcus doing his project?

....

2 What is Marcus' project about?

....

3 Where does Marcus write about his project every day?

....

4 How many minutes can Marcus spend on the computer each day?

....

5 Who is laughing at Marcus?

....

6 Who misses talking to his/her friends?

....

7 Who often spends the holiday without technology?

....

8 Who doesn't use a computer on Saturdays?

....

A tech-free holiday – *can I do it?*

A report by Marcus Jones

It's the start of our one-week school holiday in May. I'm getting ready for a holiday without technology! That means no mobile phones, no video games and no YouTube. I'm doing it as part of a school project. For the project, we're looking at lives of teenagers fifty years ago. So our homework is to spend the school holiday without technology and write a daily diary about it. We spend fifteen minutes writing about our opinions and feelings in our school diary every day and then we upload our diary entries to the school blog. That's the only time we can use technology!

It's only 4 p.m. on Saturday and I'm already missing my phone. It feels strange. My sister is sitting next to me on the sofa. She's texting her friends and laughing at me! My family think I can't live without technology. I want to show them they're wrong! How is everyone else doing?

Dan, 15   Add message | Report

I'm finding it easy at the moment. I play football every Saturday and so I don't usually play on my computer anyway.

Alexandra, 16   Add message | Report

I'm feeling a bit bored! I miss chatting to my friends online. I can't believe it's only day 1!

Sienna, 15   Add message | Report

It's easy for me because I'm staying with family in Wales for the holiday. We come every May on holiday. The house doesn't have wi-fi and my mobile has no signal here. I'm writing this in a café in the town. Our holidays here are always technology-free!

4 Find words in the report that have these meanings.

1 computers, mobile phones and the internet are examples of this: ....

2 what you think about something or someone: ....

3 a website where people write about their experiences, opinions and feelings: ....

4 unusual: ....

5 your mobile phone needs this to send and receive information: ....

6 a place where you can have lunch, coffee or tea: ....

GRAMMAR

talking about now

1 Complete the table with the *-ing* form of the verbs.

get	1 ....
write	2 ....
have	3 ....
sit	4 ....
make	5 ....
win	6 ....
teach	7 ....
study	8 ....

2 Put the words in the correct order to make sentences.

1 some photos / are / Kirsty and Tim / looking at

....

2 watching a film / am / with my friends / I

....

3 writing / Eddie / in his school diary / is

....

4 a science experiment / are / the students / doing

....

5 George / is / his homework / doing

....

6 about space / we / reading / are / on the computer

....

7 and I / project / are / doing / together / Emma

....

8 waiting / am / for my friend James / I

....

3 Choose the correct words to complete the sentences.

1 My mobile phone **isn't / aren't** working.
2 Penny **is / are** waiting for us.
3 My cousins **isn't / aren't** watching a film.
4 Stefan **'s / are** feeling ill.
5 The children **is / are** playing video games.
6 It **aren't / isn't** raining now.
7 We **isn't / aren't** watching TV right now.
8 Amy and her friend **is / are** doing a project for school.
9 Lisa and Mike **is / are** playing a board game.
10 Lee **isn't / aren't** having a good time.

4 🔊 2.1 Complete the conversation with the present continuous form of the verbs in brackets. Use short forms where possible. Listen and check your answers.

A: Hi, Sam. What **1** .... you .... (do)?
B: Hi, Holly. I **2** .... (wait) for my brother. He's always late!
A: Is that your guitar? **3** .... you .... (learn) to play?
B: Yes, I am. I have lessons every Tuesday.
A: **4** .... Mrs Morgan .... (teach) you?
B: Usually yes, but she **5** .... (not feel) well. Mr Dunbar **6** .... (do) all the music lessons this week.

5 Look at the picture and complete the sentences. Use these phrases.

drink / a cup of tea   eat / a cake   read / a book
sleep / on the rug   talk / on the phone   ~~watch / TV~~

Toby _is watching TV_ .
1 Toby's sister Olivia ....
2 Toby's mum ....
3 Toby's dad ....
4 Toby's grandma ....
5 Toby's dog and cat ....

VOCABULARY

technology

1 Read the clues and complete the crossword.

Across

3 the part of a computer you use to type words

4 a telephone you can use anywhere

6 something you use to move around the screen of a computer

Down

1 the part of a computer you look at to read information

2 you listen to music through these

5 a small computer that you can move easily

2 Match 1–6 with A–F to make sentences.

1 Every Saturday Becky chats ......

2 Ben and Alex stream ......

3 I'm listening to music with ......

4 Mia is sending ......

5 It's cheap and easy to download ......

6 They're looking ......

A my new headphones.

B music with this app.

C online with her cousin in Canada.

D at a website about a music festival.

E films together in the evenings.

F an email to her teacher about her homework.

3 Choose the correct answer, A, B or C.

1 This café ...... free wi-fi.

   A gives   **B** has   **C** does

2 This laptop is great for listening to music as it has brilliant ....

   A speakers   **B** screens   **C** webcams

3 I'm making a film with my new ...... camera.

   A internet   **B** wi-fi   **C** digital

4 Go to the website and ...... on this link for information.

   A click   **B** switch   **C** turn

5 Have you got a ...... ? I need to give my homework to the teacher tomorrow.

   A mouse   **B** printer   **C** webcam

4 🔊 2.2 Complete the sentences from an interview with these words. Listen and check your answers.

downloads	laptop	online	send	stream	tablet

www.lunaradio.com

1 My brother and I have a .... each. We often .... emails and .... films.

2 My dad doesn't like computers, but he does have a .... He needs it for work.

3 My mum uses her mobile phone all the time. She often .... music and chats to my aunty ....

4 You can leave a message on the radio station website. Our address is ....

Extend

5 Choose the correct words to complete the letter.

Dear students,

All homework is now online. You need to download the **¹internet / software** to use the online homework at home. **²Check / See** online every day to find homework from your teacher. **³Switch on / Open** the file your teacher leaves for your class and do the exercises. When you finish your homework, **⁴save / look after** your file and send it to your teacher.

Today's homework is: **⁵Look for / Search** the internet for information about our solar system and **⁶create / do** a file with ten questions to ask the rest of the class.

Please speak to me if you have any problems.

Mr Harrison

LISTENING

1 Read the questions in Ex 2. What kind of information do you need to listen for (e.g. a time, a date, an object, a number)?

2 🌐 🔊 2.3 Listen and for each question, choose the correct picture.

1 What does Holly want for her birthday?

2 Which man is Harriet's computer teacher?

3 What is Maisy writing about for her homework?

4 What time can Evie call Charlie?

5 How much are the speakers?

3 🔊 2.4 Listen again and answer the questions.

1 Why does Holly not like her laptop?

....

2 What do we know about the age of Harriet's teacher?

....

3 What does Maisy want a printer for?

....

4 Where's Charlie's brother?

....

5 Why doesn't Adam buy the speakers?

....

present simple and present continuous

4 Choose the correct answer, A, B or C.

1 Callum .... tennis every day, but he's not playing today because he's ill.

   A doesn't play   **B** plays   **C** isn't playing

2 Mrs Crewe .... us today because our teacher is ill.

   A is teaching   **B** teach   **C** teaches

3 Tom .... with his aunt this week. His parents are on a business trip.

   A is staying   **B** stays   **C** staying

4 Jack usually .... home for lunch. Today he's having lunch with his friends.

   A is going   **B** are going   **C** goes

5 My mum usually .... us to school, but today we're walking to school.

   A drive   **B** drives   **C** 's driving

5 Match 1–5 with A–E to make sentences.

1 Matt normally texts his friends in the morning, ...

2 I'm walking to school this week ....

3 They normally love going to the cinema, ...

4 I want to do my school work on the computer, ...

5 Ella's staying at home today ....

A but they're not enjoying this film.

B because she doesn't feel very well.

C but his phone isn't working today.

D but my sister's using it at the moment.

E because my bike needs a new wheel.

6 🌐 Read the email and write the correct answer in each gap. Write one word for each gap.

Hi Georgia,

How are you? ....*Are*........ you having a good holiday? I'm staying at my grandparents' house for the holidays. They ¹........................ in the mountains. It's an amazing place. There ²........................ lots of things to do here. Every day we ³........................ fishing or horse-riding. It's great fun. I can't phone you because there isn't a signal for my mobile phone at my grandparents' house. I'm ⁴........................ this email in an internet café in town. My grandparents are ⁵........................ some shopping. I hope you're ⁶........................ a good time.

See you next week!
Anna

SPEAKING

1 Look at the pictures. Complete the sentences with these words.

behind	between	in front of	next to	opposite

1 The boy is standing .... a door.
2 The boy is standing .... a cat.
3 The boy is standing .... a girl and a cat.
4 The girl is standing .... a tree.
5 The girl is sitting .... a boy.

2 Ella is talking about a photo on her mobile phone. Look at the picture and complete the text with these words.

behind	between	in front of	next to	opposite

This is a picture of my friends and me. We're at Tom's birthday party. I'm the girl with short hair and a rainbow T-shirt sitting on the right. I'm sitting **¹**..........................my best friend Freya. Her brother, Owen, is sitting next to her and **²**.......................... me. He's got short dark hair and is wearing a jumper. My brother, Joe, is standing **³**.......................... Owen. Joe's wearing a silly party hat! The boy **⁴**.......................... the window is Andy. He's laughing at a funny joke. The boy **⁵**.......................... Joe and Andy is Matt. He's really funny! He's always dancing.

3 🔊 2.5 Complete the conversation with the present simple or present continuous form of the verbs in brackets. Listen and check your answers.

A: **¹**.......................... you .... (go) home now?
B: No, I'm going to my cousin's house.
I **²**.......................... (stay) with him at the moment.
A: Really? Why?
B: My parents **³**.......................... (do) some work in the house. There **⁴**.......................... (be) no electricity, so the internet **⁵**.......................... (not work). I'm using my cousin's computer for my homework.
A: Where's your sister staying?
B: She's at my cousin's house, too. They **⁶**.......................... (live) in a really big house, so there's an extra bedroom for me and my sister.

WRITING

1 Match sentences 1–6 with sentences A-F.

1 I love my tablet. ....
2 I love listening to music on my phone. ....
3 I've got thirty books on my e-book. ....
4 I love taking photos on my phone. ....
5 My dad bought me a laptop. ....
6 I play on my Xbox with my sister after school. ....

A I usually share my photos on social media.
B I never read paper books now.
C I've got about 1,500 songs on it.
D We play the games on the TV in our bedroom.
E I really enjoy making videos of my friends with it.
F I watch films on it all the time.

2 Complete the sentences with these words.

game   maps   messaging   music
social media   translator

1 I use my .... app to search for words in different languages.
2 My brother's excited because the new version of his favourite Xbox .... comes out tomorrow.
3 I use a .... app to speak to my friends when they are away on holiday.
4 Apparently, teenagers check their .... every two hours.
5 I haven't got GPS but we can use the .... on my phone to find the hotel.
6 Which .... app do you use for streaming your favourite songs?

3 Choose the correct words to complete the text.

My favourite gadget is my laptop. It's black ¹**and / because / but** pink. I love my laptop ²**and / but / because** I can use it anywhere. It's got a webcam, ³**because / but / and** I don't use it very much. I love chatting to my friends online ⁴**and / because / but** looking at all my photos. I enjoy watching films on it ⁵**and / but / because** it has a big screen. I can't live without it!

4 Complete the sentences with *and, but* or *because*.

1 I like playing games .... they are fun.
2 My favourite apps are Snapchat, Instagram .... Facebook.
3 My maps app helps me find new places .... doesn't tell me the time.
4 I sometimes stream films .... it's cheaper than the cinema.
5 My music app works offline .... my translator app needs the internet.
6 For my birthday, I want a tablet .... some new speakers.

5 Read the text and answer the questions.

Hi, my name's Oli. I love 'Minecraft'. It's a great game and now it even has an app! I use it all the time. It's great to play it when I'm waiting for the bus. I like playing against people from other countries. I also use it at weekends when I'm relaxing at home. I like showing my mum and dad all the cool things I build.

1 What kind of app does Oli like?   ....
2 Why does Oli like the app?   ....
3 When does Oli use the app?   ....

6 Write about your favourite piece of technology (phone, tablet, e-book, laptop, etc.) Describe it, explain why you like it and where and when you like using it. Write 25 words or more.

UNIT CHECK

1 **Choose the correct words to complete the conversations.**

1 **A:** Can we watch the film at your house?

   B: Sorry, our TV isn't working and my brother's using the **laptop / webcam**.

2 **A:** Don't eat your lunch at the computer! You're dropping food on the **keyboard / screen**.

   B: OK, Dad. Sorry.

3 **A:** Max, your dinner's ready. Put your **speakers / mobile phone** down, please.

   B: OK, but can I send one quick text to Harry, please, Mum?

4 **A:** Can you play music on your laptop?

   B: Yes, but the **keyboard / speakers** aren't very good, so the music's not very loud.

5 **A:** Why are you closing the curtains?

   B: The sun's shining on my laptop and I can't read the information on the **screen / mouse**.

6 **A:** How do I open this file?

   B: Move the arrow on top of it and then click the button on the **speakers / mouse**.

7 **A:** My **webcam / printer** isn't working and I need to make three copies of my project. Can I use yours?

   B: Sure. Here's some paper.

2 **Match sentences 1–6 with sentences A–F.**

1 My brother's got a new tablet. ....

2 Rachel never sends emails to her friends. ....

3 My brother's not asleep. ....

4 I always buy my clothes online. ....

5 It's important to save your files. ....

6 I'm not sure how much the tickets cost. ....

A She always sends texts.

B I can check online.

C This is my favourite website for jeans.

D It's got a great camera on it.

E You don't want to lose all your work!

F He's listening to music with his headphones.

3 **Choose the correct answer, A, B or C.**

1 I sit .... Jack in English class.

   A above   **B** next to   **C** under

2 The printer is on the table, ... the laptop and the paper.

   A between   **B** inside   **C** outside

3 Our house is .... the park.

   A under   **B** between   **C** opposite

4 You can't see Sam. She's sitting .... you.

   A behind   **B** in front of   **C** next to

5 The plane flew high .... our heads.

   A below   **B** between   **C** above

6 Harriet's staying .... today because she's not feeling very well.

   A above   **B** inside   **C** between

4 **Complete the sentences with the present continuous form of the verbs in brackets.**

1 Nicky's not here. She .... (chat) online in the other room.

2 Andy .... (download) information for his project.

3 They .... (not download) music.

4 .... Rebecca .... (stream) a film?

5 .... you .... (check) the price of the cinema times online?

6 I .... (not use) my new webcam.

5 **Complete the sentences with the present simple or present continuous form of these verbs.**

chat   click   have   listen   send   stream

1 Mia .... online to her friends in Dubai at the moment.

2 This shop .... free wi-fi for its customers.

3 You .... on this link for more information about the club.

4 Lily and Jake aren't doing their homework. They .... a film on Jake's new laptop.

5 Can you wait a minute? I .... an email to my teacher.

6 I always .... to music on my phone.

REVIEW: UNITS 1–2

1 Choose the correct words to complete the sentences.

1 Can I use your **laptop** / **headphones**, please? I want to send an email to my sister.

2 Ella's having a **singing** / **cooking** lesson. She wants to be a pop star!

3 Eric can play **chess** / **the keyboard**. He loves music.

4 I **stream** / **surf** all my music from this website.

5 This **cartoon** / **comic** is about a school. It's on Channel 5 every day for half an hour.

6 I can't read my emails because the sun's shining on the computer **mouse** / **screen**.

2 Put the words in the correct order to make sentences.

1 after school / play / we / usually / board games / don't

....

2 always / I / from / stream / this website / my music

....

3 never / computer games / they / at school / play

....

4 chat / Alistair and Tim / don't / online / often

....

5 in the evenings / usually / on her laptop / works / my mum

....

6 sometimes / my dad / to school / me / drives

....

7 get up / always / don't / late / on Sundays / I

....

3 Complete the conversation with the present simple or present continuous form of the verbs in brackets. Use short forms where possible.

A: What ¹.................... (you/do)?

B: I ².................... (paint) a picture of my mum.

A: Is it for school?

B: No, it's for the art club. I ³.................... (go) every Wednesday.

A: Oh, right. ⁴.................... (be) it good fun?

B: Yes, I ⁵.................... (love) it. We ⁶.................... (learn) to paint faces at the moment.

A: ⁷.................... you .... (draw) as well?

B: Yes, we ⁸.................... (do) different kinds of art every week.

A: Great! Can I join?

4 Look at the pictures and make sentences with these words.

above	in front of	inside	next to	outside	under

1 the clock / be / the shelf

....

....

2 it / rain

....

....

3 the boy / sit / the TV

....

....

4 the cat / sleep / the table

....

....

5 the mobile phone / be / the bag

....

....

....

6 the boy / stand / the girl

....

....

5 ⓔ Read the text and write the correct answer in each gap. Write one word for each gap.

NEW TECHNOLOGY CLUB!

Are you ¹.................... for a new hobby? We have ².................... answer for you! Holly Lane Library ³.................... starting a new technology club. There are lots of activities: you can ⁴.................... video games or you can learn ⁵.................... to make your own games. There is a full list of activities ⁶.................... our website. You can also learn ⁷.................... to make your own blogs and vlogs. We have more information ⁸.................... our website – just click on the 'info' link. The club is free but there are only twenty places. We hope to see you soon!

3 The right answer

READING

1 Complete the sentences with these words. There are two extra words.

| bored | borrowed | desk | facts | notes | relax | subject | useful |

1 I'm always really .... in maths. I don't find it interesting.

2 In history it's important to remember lots of ....

3 This book is really .... It helps me with my English.

4 Jack usually sits at his .... to do his homework.

5 Mia .... my pen because she didn't have one.

6 I can't read my .... because my writing is so small.

2 Read the article quickly. Are the sentences true (T) or false (F)?

1 The article is about Bea's school. ....

2 The article tells us about a different way of teaching. ....

3 The article describes an unusual teacher. ....

Playing basketball in a science lesson?
by Bea Forrester

Yesterday I visited a school with a very different way of teaching science. I arrived at the school and the headteacher, Ms Ross, took me to Class 4B's science lesson. I thought it was strange that Ms Ross didn't take me to the science lab. Instead, she took me to the school gym. I looked through the window and it looked like a PE lesson but it wasn't. It was a science lesson about the human body.

At the start of the lesson, the students ran around the gym and threw basketballs to each other. After ten minutes, the teacher told them to stop. The students went to the end of the gym and sat down. They sat at tables, but there were no books or pens. The teacher taught them science only with a whiteboard and her laptop.

After eight minutes of teaching, the students left their tables. They picked up the basketballs and started their ten minutes of exercise again. This happened three times. Each time the students only sat and learned science for eight minutes. The students at the school learned better and faster like this. The students remembered more information with the ten-minute breaks and exercise.

So what did I think? Well, it felt strange at first and I didn't think it was a good idea, but I soon changed my opinion. I learned a lot from the lesson – and it was a lot of fun!

3 ⓔ Read the article again. For each question, choose the correct answer.

1 Why was Bea surprised?

  A The lesson was in an unusual place.

  B The headteacher took her to a PE lesson.

  C The science lab looked strange.

2 The students learned science without

  A classroom furniture.

  B technology.

  C books.

3 The students played with the basketballs

  A only at the start of the lesson.

  B during the whole lesson.

  C at certain times in the lesson.

4 Why did students only sit for eight minutes?

  A They found science difficult.

  B The breaks helped them learn.

  C They wanted to play basketball.

5 What's Bea's opinion of the science lesson she saw?

  A She now thinks it's a good way to learn.

  B She still thinks it's a strange way of teaching.

  C She thinks it's a bad idea.

4 Choose the correct words to complete the sentences.

1 Our teacher wants to learn a new **way** / **type** of teaching Maths.

2 Mr Briggs is the **chief teacher** / **headteacher** in our school.

3 Can you **throw** / **fly** that ball to me, please?

4 We always have **fun** / **funny** in Mrs Evan's class.

5 What are you cooking? It has a **strange** / **high** smell.

6 I'm really tired. Can we have a short **stop** / **break**, please?

GRAMMAR

past simple

1 Match the questions (1–6) with the answers (A–F).

1 Did Madeleine have a good English lesson? ....

2 How much was it? ....

3 Did you get a good mark in your exam? ....

4 Where was your sport lesson today? ....

5 Did Jake and Sonia have lunch at school? ....

6 When did you leave school yesterday? ....

A At 3.15 p.m. **D** £2.99.

B Yes, she did. **E** Yes, I did.

C No, they didn't. **F** In the gym.

2 Complete the sentences with *was/were* or *wasn't/ weren't*.

1 It .... Jonathan's first day at school today. He really enjoyed it.

2 I usually enjoy my lunch in the school café, but today the food .... very nice.

3 I don't usually like maths, but my lesson .... really good today.

4 Jacob and Emily .... at school today. They're not very well.

5 My English homework .... very difficult today. I finished it quickly.

6 I got a really good mark in my history exam. My parents .... really happy.

3 Complete the table.

infinitive	past simple
go	**1** ....
2	spoke
write	**3** ....
4	made
eat	**5** ....
6	saw

4 Complete the sentences with the past simple form of the verbs in brackets.

1 We .... (have) a maths exam yesterday.

2 I .... (not hear) what the teacher said.

3 Martha .... (get) a good mark in the test.

4 We .... (write) a story in class.

5 The children .... (not wear) school uniform at primary school yesterday.

6 Tom .... (forget) his homework last Friday.

5 🔊 3.1 Complete the conversation with the past simple form of the verbs in brackets. Listen and check your answers.

A: Hi, Eric. I **1** .... (have) a great day at school today!

B: Oh hi, Sarah. I **2** .... (not see) you before school this morning.

A: I know. I **3** .... (arrive) late. Anyway, a new teacher **4** .... (teach) us Spanish today.

B: Oh, yes, Miss Rodriguez. I **5** .... (meet) her yesterday.

A: She **6** .... (bring) lots of different Spanish food to try. We also **7** .... (listen) to some Spanish music. It was so much fun!

B: That sounds cool.

6 Complete the text with the past simple form of these verbs.

> begin finish go live love not be not have

My Greek school

When I was thirteen, we **1** .... in Greece for a year. My school in Greece was called 'Gymnasio'. My school day **2** .... the same as in the UK. In my Greek school, lessons **3** .... at 8.15 a.m. and **4** .... at 1.45 p.m. The school **5** .... a school café. Everyone **6** .... home for lunch. I **7** .... the school summer holidays in Greece. They were three months long!

VOCABULARY

school

1 Match the school subjects (1–8) with the pictures (A–H).

1 maths ....
2 DT ....
3 history ....
4 biology ....

5 geography ....
6 chemistry ....
7 physics ....
8 PE ....

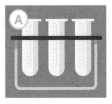 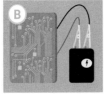 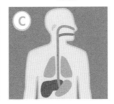

2 Match these words/phrases with the verbs (1–5).

a-good-mark   a football shirt   a language   an exam
a school uniform   bored   home   homework
in your notebook   on the board   Spanish

1 get a good mark ....
2 have/do ....
3 learn ....
4 wear ....
5 write ....

3 Complete the sentences with the past simple form of the verbs in Ex 3.

1 I .... a good mark in my maths test.
2 I .... my homework on Friday evening.
3 I .... a maths exam last week.
4 I .... a football shirt for sport.
5 I .... bored in the history lesson.
6 I .... an answer on the board yesterday.

4 Read the blog post. Choose the correct answer for each gap.

SCHOOL IS COOL!

I like going to school because I see my best friends there. All the students wear a <u>uniform</u> at my school. I don't sit in the same **1**...... all day. We move for each lesson. I never remember what lesson I have, so I'm always looking at my **2**...... ! My favourite lesson is **3**...... . I go to France on holiday sometimes and I like speaking the language. Our teacher is really cool and he often draws funny pictures on the **4**...... . We **5**...... an exam last week. This morning we got our **6**...... . I was really happy because I got 19/20.

	A	**B**	**C**
	A uniform	**B** bag	**C** glasses
1	**A** table	**B** classroom	**C** desk
2	**A** teacher	**B** pencil case	**C** timetable
3	**A** French	**B** geography	**C** English
4	**A** board	**B** desk	**C** pen
5	**A** wrote	**B** had	**C** gave
6	**A** classroom	**B** timetable	**C** marks

Extend

5 Complete the sentences with these words.

classmate   dictionary   eraser   school rule   science
staff room

1 The teachers spend their break in the ....
2 Check the meaning of this word in the ....
3 Jack is my .... We sit together at school.
4 You can use an .... when you make a mistake with a pencil.
5 You can't use your phone at school. It's a ....
6 Biology and chemistry are .... subjects.

LISTENING

1 🔊 3.2 **Listen to Ava and Ben talking about school. Answer the questions.**

1 What subject is Ava doing for homework?

....

2 What kind of schools did Ava learn about from the film?

....

3 Are Ava and Ben in the same class? How do you know?

....

2 e 🔊 3.3 **Listen again. For each question, choose the correct answer.**

1 Yesterday, Ava watched a film about schools in
  A Bangladesh.
  B Argentina.
  C Russia.

2 Ava thought the film was
  A surprising.
  B interesting.
  C boring.

3 The schools in the film open
  A in dry weather.
  B all of the year.
  C in wet weather.

4 Ben thought the school computers might use
  A solar power.
  B electricity.
  C battery power.

5 Ben would like to go to a boat school
  A once.
  B all the time.
  C instead of his school.

3 🔊 3.4 **Listen again and complete the sentences.**

1 Ava is studying education around ....

2 The film Ava watched yesterday was about .... schools.

3 In Bangladesh the normal schools close in the .... season.

4 The boat is also like a school ....

5 The boat uses energy from the ....

6 Each boat has a classroom for about .... students.

7 Ben prefers schools on ....

past simple questions and short answers

4 **Complete the short answers.**

1 A: Was Helena at school today?
   B: Yes, ...

2 A: Were Leo and Jake in the school café at 1 p.m.?
   B: No, ...

3 A: Was your homework difficult?
   B: Yes, ...

4 A: Were your notebooks at home?
   B: Yes, ...

5 A: Was Andy late for the lesson?
   B: No, ...

6 A: Were the exam results good?
   B: No, ...

5 **Complete the questions with the past simple form of these verbs.**

close	do	learn	play	read	wear

1 .... you .... your homework before dinner yesterday?

2 .... your parents .... a school uniform when they were your age?

3 .... your friends .... football at school last week?

4 .... you .... a good book last month?

5 .... your school .... because of snow last winter?

6 .... your grandma .... English at school?

6 **Complete the email with these words.**

did	didn't	had	saw	took	was (x2)	went

Hi Billie,

How ¹..................... your school trip? ².....................
you have a good time? I came back from my school
history trip yesterday. We ³..................... to London.
We ⁴..................... a really good time. We visited
lots of old places. My favourite place ⁵.....................
the Tower of London. We also went to Buckingham
Palace, but we ⁶..................... see the Queen!
I ⁷..................... lots of photos for my school project.
We also went to the cinema in Leicester Square one
evening. We ⁸..................... a really good film.

Speak soon,
Helen

3 The right answer

SPEAKING

1 Choose the correct words to complete the questions.

A Who / What was the first person you met at school? ......

B Why / What was your first lesson? ......

C How / Why were you worried? ......

D How / Where did you feel? ......

E How many / How much people did you already know at the school? ......

F Why / Where did you live before? ......

2 🔊 3.5 **Listen to Rebecca talking to Max. Put the questions in Ex 1 in the correct order (1–6).**

3 Put the words in the correct order to make questions.

1 your maths exam / was / difficult today?

....

2 finish / you / your history homework / did?

....

3 a good mark / did / get / in his biology test / David?

....

4 the answer on the board / the teacher / did / write?

....

5 your library books / were / in your school bag?

....

6 have / Clare and Mark / lunch in the school café / did?

....

7 late / were / for school / yesterday / you?

....

8 walk / the boys / did / today / to school?

....

4 Complete the past simple questions. Write one word in each gap.

1 What .... you do last Saturday?

2 What .... you learn in your first lesson today?

3 .... did you speak to first this morning?

4 Where .... your parents yesterday evening?

5 .... did you have lunch yesterday?

6 When .... the last time you swam?

5 Answer the questions in Ex 4.

1 ....

2 ....

3 ....

4 ....

5 ....

6 ....

6 🔊 3.6 **Complete the conversations with these words. Listen and check your answers.**

classroom   gym   library   office   school café
science lab

1 A: Are you having lunch in the .... ?

B: No, I'm going home for lunch today.

2 A: Why are you wearing your sports shorts, Danny? We don't have sports today.

B: I've got basketball practice in the ....

3 A: Where are we having geography today?

B: .... 12B. It's next to the gym.

4 A: What are all those books for?

B: For my history project. I'm taking them back to the ....

5 A: Who do I give my form for the school trip to?

B: You give it to the school secretary. She's in the ....

6 A: Where are you going?

B: To the .... I've got chemistry with Ms Yates.

7 🔊 3.7 **Listen and repeat.**

1 A: Were you at school last Friday?

B: Yes, I was.

2 A: Was Pippa in your class last year?

B: No, she wasn't.

3 A: Were we late yesterday?

B: No, we weren't.

4 A: Was your science lesson interesting?

B: Yes, it was.

8 🔊 3.8 **Listen, speak and record. Listen back and compare.**

WRITING

1 Complete the sentences with these adjectives.

---

boring   brilliant   different   fun   interesting   loud

---

1 The film we watched in our geography lesson was really
.... I nearly fell asleep!

2 Can you turn your music down, please? It's really ....

3 I got .... marks in my exams. My parents were really
pleased.

4 This is a really .... book. I read it in two days.

5 My new school is very .... from my last school, but
I really like it.

6 Our school trip last week was great .... I can't wait for
the next one!

2 e Read Amy's email to Theo. Write the correct answer in each
gap. Write one word for each gap.

Hi Theo,

We went on a school trip ¹.......................... York today. It was great
fun! First, we visited the castle. Then we went to ²..........................
castle gift shop. There were some nice things, but I didn't buy
anything. It was all too expensive. After the castle we went
³.......................... a short walk by the river. At lunchtime we had
a picnic next ⁴.......................... the river. After lunch we went to
a really cool Viking museum. Before we left York, we went on
⁵.......................... short boat trip. I was really pleased ⁶..........................
I was so tired from all the walking!

Amy

3 Write the words and phrases Amy uses to
show what order things happened in.

.... First ....

1 ....

2 ....

3 ....

4 ....

5 ....

4 Put the words in the correct order to
make sentences.

A I / after / lesson / went / home / my

....

B I / woke up / first / six o'clock / at

....

C went / school / I / then / to

....

D school / had / lesson / piano / I / after / a

....

5 Put the sentences in Ex 4 (A–D) in the
correct order (1–4) to make a story.

1 ....   **2** ....   **3** ....   **4** ....

6 e Write a description of a school trip for
a school magazine. Use the past simple
and words and phrases for ordering
events. Write 25 words or more.

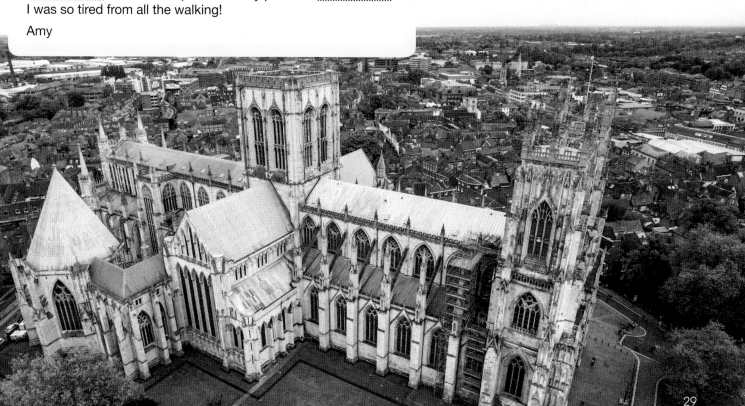

29

UNIT CHECK

1 Complete the school subjects in the sentences.

1 We painted a picture of some fruit in a........................ class today.

2 Marc learned about the ancient Greeks in h........................ .

3 My p........................ lesson was all about space.

4 We learned the phrase 'c'est la vie' in our F........................ lesson.

5 Kiera played tennis in her s........................ lesson.

6 We made a clock in D........................ last month.

2 Choose the correct answer A, B or C.

1 Did you have maths this morning?
  A Yes, I had.
  B Yes, we did.
  C Yes, you did.

2 Did Lara have lunch in the school café today?
  A Yes, she did.
  B Yes, she does.
  C Yes, she have.

3 Was Emma at school yesterday?
  A No, she didn't.
  B No, she wasn't.
  C No, she weren't.

4 Were the books on the shelf?
  A Yes, they were.
  B Yes, they did.
  C Yes, they was.

5 Did everyone pass the biology exam?
  A Yes, they do.
  B Yes, they did.
  C Yes, they done.

6 Did Freddie's teacher go on the school trip?
  A No, they didn't.
  B No, he wasn't.
  C No, she didn't.

3 Complete the conversation with these words.

did   didn't   enjoy   see   want   wore

A: Hi, William. Did you ¹........................ 'No School Uniform' day?

B: Yes, I ²........................ . I loved wearing cap and hoodie all day!

A: I know! I didn't ³........................ to put on my school uniform this morning.

B: Did you ⁴........................ my maths teacher, Mr Hill, yesterday?

A: No, I ⁵........................ . Why?

B: He ⁶........................ a school uniform to school! He's so funny!

A: That's brilliant! My teachers didn't do anything like that.

4 Make past simple questions.

1 Mr Sampson / be / in the staff room / at lunchtime?
....

2 Georgia / learn / Chinese / at school?
....

3 the children / be / at school / today?
....

4 Lisa / wear / her new football shirt ?
....

5 Emilia and Max / get / good marks / for their DT projects?
....

6 you / be / in the library / after lunch
....

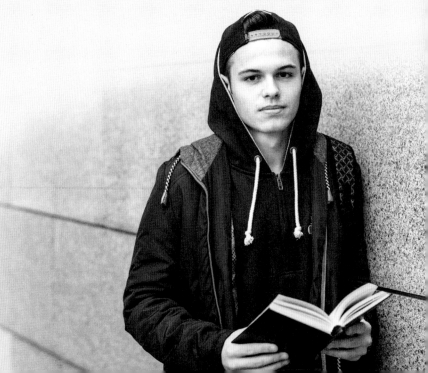

REVIEW: UNITS 1–3

1 Match 1–6 with A–F to make sentences.

1 Ella often goes on ......
2 My music sounds great ......
3 Have you got a ruler? ......
4 My little brother loves ......
5 I can't open this ......
6 My desk is between ......

A watching cartoons on TV.
B the bookcase and the cupboard.
C sleepovers at her friend's house at the weekend.
D file. Can you help me?
E I want to draw a straight line.
F with my new speakers.

2 Complete the sentences with the present simple, present continuous or past simple form of the verbs in brackets.

1 Every Saturday morning Emma .... (have) dancing lessons.
2 I .... (come) home at about 5 p.m. yesterday.
3 Can you be quiet? I .... (do) my homework.
4 Archie .... (not see) his friends last weekend.
5 I like your football shirt. .... (be) it new?
6 Miss Arch .... (not teach) us today because she's ill.

3 Choose the correct words to complete the questions.

1 Did / Were the students loud in class?
2 Do / Were you get up early at the weekend?
3 What / Where did you do last summer?
4 Was / Were she at school today?
5 Are / Did you glad you got a good mark?
6 Were / Did they go to the gym after school?

4 Complete the text. Write one word for each gap.

Today **1**..................... the last day before summer.
First, I went to music class and we **2**.....................
the guitar. Then, I **3**..................... to chemistry
class and we **4**..................... a rocket. It was
amazing! At lunchtime I went to the school café
and **5**..................... 'Happy Birthday' to Dan. In the
afternoon, we all **6**..................... a yoga class.

5 Put the words in the correct order to make sentences.

1 this week / isn't / my brother / sport / doing
....
2 my best friend / I / two years ago / met
....
3 never / my dad / cakes or biscuits / bakes
....
4 lots of music / Oliver / to his new phone / downloaded
....
5 play / we / at the weekend / board games / sometimes
....
6 the tree / Grace / is / behind / sitting
....

6 **e** Read the article. Choose the correct answer for each gap.

LEARNING YOUR OWN WAY

What are your interests? Do you like **1**...... video games or listening to music? Some schools are learning that doing certain activities helps students learn. Many schools use technology in the **2**...... now; it's not a new idea. Many schools use special **3**...... on computers to teach school subjects. However, did you know that in some schools, **4**...... play games on a tablet? It's the first activity of the day on the timetable. This is because teachers found that a brain-training **5**...... on the tablet helped children learn better. In other schools, teachers play hip hop music and even rap to teach subjects. They put the classwork to music and students learn the information as songs. In these schools your homework is sometimes to **6**...... to music!

1 A doing   **B** playing   **C** going
2 A classroom   **B** DT   **C** webcam
3 A internet   **B** wi-fi   **C** software
4 A persons   **B** pupils   **C** staff
5 A file   **B** game   **C** work
6 A listen   **B** make   **C** hear

31

READING

1 Complete the words in the sentences.

1 My sister loves looking at herself in the
m............................ .

2 I never go to markets. I prefer online
s............................ .

3 The jeans on this website are not expensive
and the d............................ is free.

4 Instead of people, this shop has
r............................ shop assistants.

5 I'm really busy. I don't have t............................
to shop.

6 These trousers are too small. Do you have
them in a larger s............................ ?

2 Read the article. Are the sentences true (T)
or false (F)?

1 Bonobos customers can only look at the
clothes in a Bonobos shop. ....

2 You can only buy Bonobos clothes online. ....

3 Most online shoppers in the USA try clothes
on in a shop before they buy online. ....

4 Shop assistants in guideshops never work
with money. ....

5 Guideshops always have a customer's size in
any item of clothing. ....

6 Guideshops are often very big shops. ....

3 Find words/phrases in the article with the
opposite meaning.

1 a few (para 1)   ....

2 now (para 2)   ....

3 after (para 2)   ....

4 never (para 3)   ....

5 everyone (para 3)   ....

6 first (para 3)   ....

7 unusual (para 4)   ....

8 the past (para 5)   ....

The shops that sell **nothing**

1 The American company Bonobos sells men's clothes and you can find Bonobos shops in many US cities. But Bonobos shops are more unusual than most shops because you can't actually buy clothes from there. Yes, you read correctly! Customers can only try on clothes in the shop. Customers then order the clothes they want online and the clothes arrive at the customer's house as soon as the next day.

2 In the past you could only see Bonobos clothes online. However, like many online shoppers, Bonobos' customers really wanted to try clothes on before buying. Do you know that nearly half of all online shoppers in the USA try things on in shops before buying them online? So Bonobos decided to give their customers a place to try on its clothes.

3 Bonobos called these places 'Guideshops'. The idea is that these guideshops help customers choose the right clothes. The shop assistants give customers advice about colour and sizes. The good thing is that you can always find your size because no one can buy the last medium size T-shirt! Also, you never have heavy shopping bags to take home with you!

4 These kinds of shops also save companies money. It's cheaper because guideshops don't need the space that 'normal' shops need. They don't need twenty large blue jumpers, they only need one. It also means they don't need to spend as much money on sending and returning lots of clothes to and from shops.

5 Is this the future of all shops – places where we 'experience' things instead of buying things?

GRAMMAR

comparative adjectives

1 Write the comparative form of these adjectives in the correct place in the table.

| bad | busy | difficult | good | interesting | pretty | quick | short |

-er	-ier	more + adjective	irregular

2 Choose the correct words to complete the sentences.

1 The jacket is **more expensive / expensiver** than the trousers.
2 The green bag is **nicer / more nice** than the red one.
3 The shop assistants are **helpfuller / more helpful** here than in the other shop.
4 Online shopping is **more easy / easier** than going to the shops.
5 The sports clothes in the market are **cheaper / more cheaper** than the ones in the sports shop.
6 The prices are **better / more good** here than in the other shop.

3 Complete the sentences with the comparative form of the adjectives in brackets.

1 Your jacket is .... (small) than mine.
2 The music in this shop is .... (bad) than in the last shop.
3 I think shopping is .... (boring) than doing homework.
4 Their shopping bags are .... (heavy) than ours.
5 This birthday card is .... (funny) than the other one.
6 This music shop is .... (big) than the one in my town.

4 Complete the questions with the comparative form of the adjectives in brackets.

1 Do you think it's .... (quick) to buy something online or in a shop?
2 Do you think it's .... (bad) to go clothes shopping with your parents?
3 Do you think shopping is .... (boring) than doing homework?
4 Are markets .... (popular) than shops in your country?
5 Do you think it's .... (hard) to choose clothes or shoes?
6 Are you .... (happy) in a shopping centre or in a sports centre?

5 Answer the questions in Ex 4.

6 🔊 4.1 Listen to the conversation between Mia and Finn. What kind of shop are they in?

7 🔊 4.2 Listen again and complete the conversation.

A: You're right, Finn. The sports clothes here are much **1**........................... than in the sports shop. I thought they only sold food here.

B: No, they sell all sorts of things, but only in the **2**........................... supermarkets like this one. The prices in the sports shop are always a lot **3**........................... than here.

A: Do you buy all your sports stuff from here?

B: Not everything. I buy my trainers from the sports shop. Their trainers are **4**........................... than the ones here. They're **5**..........................., but there's a **6**........................... choice in the sports shop.

VOCABULARY

shopping

1 Complete the sentences with these words.

> bargain   card   cash   price   receipt   sale

1 What's the .... of this bag?

2 I bought a really nice bag for £5 today. It was a real .... !

3 My mum bought the concert tickets online with her ....

4 Have you got the .... for my T-shirt, Mum? I want to return it to the shop.

5 Have you got any .... ? They don't take cards in this shop.

6 My favourite shop has a .... this weekend. Everything in the shop is half price!

2 Match 1–6 with A–F to make sentences.

1 I'm saving   **A** us nothing. It was free entry.

2 My dad paid   **B** a new dress for my party.

3 It cost   **C** all of his money on computer games yesterday.

4 I bought   **D** his bike to a friend.

5 Thomas sold   **E** the bill in the restaurant.

6 He spent   **F** my money for my holiday.

3 Choose the correct words to complete the sentences.

1 My new jeans were a bargain. They only **paid / cost** £15.

2 Fiona's **saving / collecting** her birthday money because she wants to buy a guitar.

3 They **bought / paid** a new computer game at the weekend.

4 Noah doesn't **buy / spend** a lot of money on music.

5 My grandma **paid / bought** for my tennis lessons.

6 How much **are / cost** these dance shoes?

4 🔊 4.3 Listen and write the prices you hear.

1 ....   **4** ....

2 ....   **5** ....

3 ....   **6** ....

5 🔊 4.4 Listen and repeat.

1 25p   **4** $40

2 €55   **5** £6.60

3 £30   **6** $0.23

6 🔊 4.5 Listen, speak and record. Listen back and compare.

Extend

7 Choose the correct words to complete the questions.

1 Do you like watching **adverts / bills** on TV?

2 Do you think it's a good idea to **rent / complain** a bicycle when you visit a new city?

3 Do you know anyone who is a **bill / manager** of a shop?

4 Do you ever **return / complain** when you're not happy with something you buy?

5 Who paid the **bill / receipt** when you last ate in a café?

6 When was the last time you **returned / replied** something to a shop?

8 Answer the questions in Ex 7.

LISTENING

1 e 🔊 **4.6 Listen and for each question, choose the correct answer.**

1 You will hear Emma talking to her grandmother about shopping. Why did Emma buy the notebook?

   A for her school work

   B for a friend's birthday present

   C for drawing pictures

2 You will hear Jack talking to his dad about some new trainers. Why does Jack want to change his new trainers?

   A They're not the correct colour.

   B They're not the right size.

   C They're from the wrong shop.

3 You will hear a brother and sister talking about plans for after school. What does Sara want Adam to do?

   A buy some milk and bread

   B wait for her at the bus stop

   C meet her outside the supermarket

4 You will hear two friends talking about which shop to go to. Which shop do the friends decide to go to next?

   A a clothes shop

   B a bookshop

   C a gift shop

5 You will hear Sue talking to her mum about a jacket she wants to buy. Why does Sue want to buy the jacket online?

   A to pay less

   B to save time

   C to get it faster

2 🔊 **4.7 Listen again. Are the sentences true (T) or false (F)?**

1 Someone gave Emma a notebook for her birthday. ......

2 Jack can only wear black trainers at school. ......

3 Adam and Sara go to the same school. ......

4 Tom is buying a present for someone in his family. ......

5 Sue wants to go shopping with her mum on Saturday. ......

superlative adjectives

3 Complete the table.

adjective	superlative
popular	¹ ....
²	worst
boring	³ ....
⁴	farthest/furthest
difficult	⁵ ....
⁶	laziest

4 Look at the pictures and complete the sentences with the superlative form of these adjectives.

dirty	expensive	happy	heavy	soft	young

1 This is the .... phone in the shop.

2 These are Joshua's .... jeans.

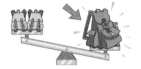 

3 My rucksack is the ....

4 Sally is the .... shop assistant.

5 This is the .... boy.

6 This is the .... toy.

5 Complete the article with the superlative form of the adjectives in brackets.

A sweet shop with a long history

¹ .... (old) sweet shop in the world is in the UK. Its name is The Oldest Sweet Shop and it's ² .... (famous) shop in the town of Pateley Bridge in England. The shop started selling sweets in 1827 and still sells sweets today. Maybe one of ³ .... (interesting) customers to the shop was a ninety-seven-year-old woman. She said the first time she bought sweets from the shop she was five years old! The shop sells ⁴ .... (amazing) sweets – from old favourites to modern sweets. It isn't ⁵ .... (large) sweet shop in the UK, but I think it's probably ⁶ .... (good)!

SPEAKING

1 **Choose the correct words to complete the questions.**

1 How much do you **buy** / **spend** on presents for your family?

2 Do you always **try on** / **pay for** sunglasses before you buy them?

3 Do you usually **save** / **spend** your money so you can buy something nice?

4 How much does your favourite video game **cost** / **sell**?

5 Do you always look at the price before you **sell** / **pay** for your food?

6 Do you ever **sell** / **spend** clothing you don't want anymore?

2 **Answer the questions in Ex 1.**

3 **Match the sentences (1–5) with the letters on the map (A–E).**

1 Turn left. ....

2 Go over the bridge. ....

3 Go past the traffic lights. ....

4 Turn right. ....

5 Go straight on. ....

4 🔊 4.8 **Listen and complete the conversations.**

1 **A:** Hi, ... you tell me .... the supermarket is, please?

   B: Yes, it's on your right, near Albert Street.

2 **A:** Excuse ...., can you tell me where the library is, ...?

   B: Sure. It's opposite the theatre.

3 **A:** .... you .... me how to get to Barron Street, please?

   B: Go straight on and it's the second street on your right.

5 **Put the words in the correct order to make sentences.**

1 you / me / can / where / the / please / cinema / is, / tell?

   ....

2 right / church / and / go / turn / past / the

   ....

3 tell / can / shops / you / me / where / the / are, / please?

   ....

4 the / and / they're / go / on / your / bridge / left / over

   ....

5 you / tell / get / can / me / to / to / Brook Street, / please / how?

   ....

6 on / straight / and / second / it's / the / go / road / on / your / right

   ....

WRITING

1 Read Ella's blog. Find these things.

1 a price ....
3 a location ....
2 a time ....
4 a name ....

My favourite shop is the sports shop in the town centre. It's called Active Buy and it's open every day from 9 a.m. to 5 p.m. The best thing is that the shop assistants are funny. The worst thing is that it's always busy at the weekend. Yesterday I went shopping with my dad and found a great bargain. I got two T-shirts for $10. I can't wait to wear them!

2 What does Ella think is good and bad about the shop?

1 good: ....
2 bad: ....

3 Match the sentences about people's favourite shops (1–8) with what they describe (A–D).

1 Music Direct is my favourite shop.
2 It sells sports clothes and equipment.
3 The best thing is that you can find real bargains.
4 It's in Istanbul.
5 My favourite shop's called Fanden.
6 I love the shop assistants – they're always so friendly.
7 You can buy clothes and shoes in this shop.
8 It's in Washington.

A where the shop is: ...., ...
B its name: ...., ...
C what it sells: ...., ...
D the best thing about it: ...., ...

4 Complete Ben's description of his favourite shop. Write one word for each gap.

Hi. My name ¹........................ Ben. My favourite shop's called Red Wheels. It's ²........................ Manchester. Red Wheels sells bicycles ³........................ skateboards. ⁴........................ best thing about this shop is the mountain bikes they sell. I love going there ⁵........................ my friends. The worst ⁶........................ about the shop is that it's always busy.

5 What do you think are the best and worst things about shops in your area? Write three good things and three bad things.

good	bad
....	....
....	....
....	....

6 Write about your favourite place in your town (cinema, café, sports centre, park, etc.). Include the name of the place, where it is, how often you go there and why you like it. Write 25 words or more.

UNIT CHECK

1 Match the questions (1–8) with the answers (A–H).

1 How much are these jeans? ....
2 Where are the customer toilets? ....
3 Have you got your receipt? ....
4 Can I pay by card? ....
5 How much is this book? ....
6 Where's the shop assistant? ....
7 Does she work here? ....
8 Did you pay the bill? ....

A Next to the men's clothing department.
B Sorry, we only take cash.
C The price is on the back of it.
D They're £59.99
E Over there. She's wearing a red uniform.
F Yes, it's in my bag.
G No, I thought you did!
H Yes, she's the manager.

2 Complete the conversation with these words.

---
bargain   closed   customer   department store
open   shop assistant   try on

A: Hi, Tara. Do you know there's a new
   ¹ .... in town?
B: Yeah, I know, Sampson's. My cousin's a
   ² .... there.
A: Really? I went there at the weekend with
   my mum. I saw some great clothes. I want
   to go back and ³ .... some jeans
   I saw.
B: OK, great. My cousin said there are
   some half-price trainers – they're a real
   ⁴ .... ! I want to get some with
   my birthday money. When do you want
   to go?
A: Well, it's ⁵ .... Monday to
   Saturday. It's only ⁶ .... on
   Sundays. Let's go tomorrow.
B: Great! Tomorrow, then. And I think for the
   first month every new ⁷ .... gets
   a free magazine.
A: Cool!

3 Complete the sentences with the comparative or superlative form of the adjectives in brackets.

1 The changing rooms here are .... (big) in the last shop.
2 Lunchtime is .... (busy) time of day at the café.
3 Your sunglasses are .... (old) mine.
4 The market is .... (cheap) the department store.
5 Martha's carrying .... (heavy) shopping bags.
6 We have this shirt in lots of colours, but black is ....
   (popular).

4 Complete the sentences. Write one word for each gap.

1 This is .... best sports shop in town.
2 Shopping online is often cheaper .... buying things at
   the shops.
3 Your trainers are .... expensive than mine.
4 The department store is busier at the weekend ....
   on weekdays.
5 It's always .... fun shopping with friends than with
   your parents.
6 This is .... worst clothes shop in my town.

5 e Read the review. Choose the correct answer for each gap.

Some people say New York is a great city for shopping. What
do I think? I think they're right! I went shopping in New York last
weekend and had the .most. amazing shopping experience.
Why? There are lots of reasons. Firstly, the shops are bigger
¹ .... the shops in my city and there is so much choice.
Secondly, the shop ² .... are friendlier than in many other places.
You can also find great ³ .... in New York. I bought ⁴ .... jeans
and they were $30 cheaper than the normal price. There are also
lots of cool ⁵ .... to stop and have lunch. My favourite is Papa
Joe's Pizzeria. They make the ⁶ .... pizzas!

	A much	B most	C more
1	A to	B from	C than
2	A assistants	B sales	C receipts
3	A cash	B bargains	C bills
4	A a	B any	C some
5	A places	B ways	C adverts
6	A good	B better	C best

REVIEW: UNITS 1–4

1 Match the words (1–6) with their meanings (A–F).

1	dictionary	**A**	a piece of paper that tells you how much to pay
2	staff room	**B**	over
3	above	**C**	a book of words and their meanings
4	brilliant	**D**	a grade for school work
5	bill	**E**	the place where teachers spend their breaks
6	mark	**F**	really good

2 Choose the correct words to complete the sentences.

1 My parents **paid / bought** my new tablet for me.

2 My cousins **have / wear** a grey uniform to school.

3 We **had / wrote** a geography exam last Monday.

4 Liam **did / got** first prize in the baking competition.

5 Sara **collects / joins** model planes in her free time.

6 I **spent / saved** all my birthday money on new speakers.

3 Complete the sentences with the correct form of these verbs.

check   collect   complain   create   download   get   take   try on

1 I'm in the changing room at the moment. I'm .... a shirt.

2 My dad wasn't happy with the food, so he .... to the café manager.

3 I .... a great photo of my friends when we went on the school trip to Paris.

4 Elliot usually starts drawing when he .... bored in class.

5 You .... a new file for every new piece of homework you do on the computer.

6 I think the bus leaves at 3.45, but can you .... online for me?

7 My cousins .... football cards. They've got 600!

8 I usually .... music from this website.

4 Choose the correct answer, A, B or C.

1 Toby's .... chess with his brother at the moment.

A play   **B** plays   **C** playing

2 Freddie .... his school bag in the classroom yesterday.

A leave   **B** left   **C** leaves

3 What mark did Annalise .... in her English exam last week?

A got   **B** get   **C** gets

4 I think this is the .... app for playing music.

A best   **B** good   **C** well

5 I can't see Tom because he's standing .... me.

A in front of   **B** behind   **C** opposite

6 Ms Pinner .... teach me science last year.

A didn't   **B** doesn't   **C** don't

5 Complete the email with the present simple, present continuous or past simple form of these verbs.

be (x2)   buy   go   sit   stop   take

Hi Harriet,

How are you? I ¹........................... shopping in London with my parents yesterday. There ²........................... lots of fantastic clothes shops. I ³........................... two new T-shirts and a pair of jeans. We ⁴........................... at a café in Covent Garden for lunch. In the afternoon we ⁵........................... my little brother to Hamley's. It ⁶........................... the world's largest toy shop! Now I ⁷........................... on the train and we're on our way home.

See you at school tomorrow.

Love,
Natalie

5 That's entertainment!

Tomorrow's stars

READING

1 Complete the sentences with these words.

box   electricity   field   popcorn   sign   staff

1 The summer cinema was in a ....
   We took a picnic and sat on the grass.
2 Lots of things in our house need .... –
   for example, the lights, the TV and the cooker.
3 My new shoes came in a red ....
4 There's a big .... on the wall and it
   says 'No mobile phones'.
5 We always eat .... at the cinema.
6 The .... in the cinema are always very
   friendly and helpful.

2 e Read the texts. For each question, choose the
correct answer.

	Henry	Isadora	Elliot
Which person learned something from a member of their family?	(A)	B	C
1 Which person never wants to sing on TV?	A	B	C
2 Which person plays a musical instrument?	A	B	C
3 Which person was at a different school last year?	A	B	C
4 Which person lives in London?	A	B	C
5 Which person did something they were afraid of?	A	B	C
6 Which person was surprised last week?	A	B	C
7 Which person wants to visit different countries?	A	B	C

A Henry Cue

I'm a pupil at Redgrave School of Performing
Arts. I love singing and dancing. I started dance
lessons when I was six. My mum and aunty
are both brilliant dancers. Actually, my aunty
taught me. I also really enjoy acting. Last
week I was performing in a theatre in
London. It was really scary. I had the biggest role in the
play and I was away from home for the first time!

B Isadora Fox

I'm fifteen years old and go to Willow School of
Music. It's in London and a short walk from my
house. I love singing and my sister plays
the guitar. We're in a band together. Our
band won a special music prize a week ago.
I couldn't believe it! Most of my friends at school
want to be famous actors on TV, but not me! I don't
want to be in front of a TV camera.

C Elliot Summers

I came to Talbot School of Music and Drama at
the start of the year. Before that I was going to
a normal high school. My favourite lessons are
acting and music. I'm lucky because a friend
of my dad's is a famous guitar player. He
taught me how to play. My dream is to
be in a rock band and play on TV shows and travel
the world.

3 Complete the sentences with adjectives from the texts.
1 I don't like to be alone in the dark after I hear a
   s........................... story.
2 They're the best dancers in the school. They're
   b........................... !
3 The Queen is f........................... . Everyone knows her face.
4 It was just a n........................... day. Nothing unusual
   happened.
5 Seven is my l........................... number.
6 I want to wear something s........................... to the party.

GRAMMAR

past continuous

1 Complete the sentences with *was, were, wasn't* or *weren't*.

1 Max .... playing his guitar yesterday evening. He was studying.

2 What .... your parents doing at 10 a.m. yesterday?

3 You .... playing football. You were listening to music in your room.

4 What .... your sister singing?

5 Sorry, I .... listening. What did you say?

2 Write short answers to the questions.

A: Was Henry sitting here? ✗

B: <u>No, he wasn't.</u>...

1 A: Were you drawing a picture of me? ✓

B: ....

2 A: Was it raining yesterday? ✗

B: ....

3 A: Were your brothers playing a video game at half past six? ✗

B: ....

4 A: Was Amy sleeping at 10 a.m.? ✓

B: ....

3 🔊 5.1 Listen and repeat the questions and answers from Ex 2.

4 🔊 5.2 Listen, speak and record. Listen back and compare.

5 Complete the sentences with the past continuous form of the verbs in brackets.

1 Maisy .... (talk) to her friend.

2 Clive .... (not watch) the film.

3 We .... (get) ready for bed.

4 You .... (not dance) at the party.

5 Rob and Isla .... (buy) tickets.

6 🔊 5.3 Complete the conversation with the past continuous form of these verbs. Listen and check your answers.

---

chat   dance   do   hide   hope   practise

A: Hi, Chloe. What **1**........................... you .... yesterday evening? I didn't see you at the party at Kim's house.

B: I was at my drama club. We **2**........................... for our show. It's next week! How was the party?

A: Oh, it was alright. I **3**........................... to friends for most of the evening!

B: **4**........................... no one ....?

A: Yes, lots of people – just not me! I **5**........................... in the kitchen! I can't dance.

B: It's a shame I couldn't go. I **6**........................... to go after drama club. But we finished late.

A: Next time! Anyway, tell me about your show.

7 Complete the questions with the past continuous form of the verbs in brackets.

1 .... you .... (have) dinner with your family at 8 p.m. last night?

2 Who .... (sit) next to you in your first lesson today?

3 .... your teacher .... (speak) to the class five minutes ago?

4 .... you .... (sleep) at 3 a.m. this morning?

5 What .... you .... (talk) about with your friends before school this morning?

6 .... it .... (rain) at 10.30 p.m. last night?

8 Answer the questions in Ex 7.

1 ....

2 ....

3 ....

4 ....

5 ....

6 ....

VOCABULARY

entertainment

1 Choose the correct words to complete the sentences.

1 I love this **romantic / science fiction** film. It's about a man and a woman who save the world from aliens.

2 This **horror film / comedy** is really funny. You won't stop laughing!

3 I'm not interested in **action / comedy** films. They're full of fighting and fast cars.

4 My brother doesn't like **romantic / action** films. He doesn't like any films about love.

5 This **animation / horror** film is about the characters from my favourite comic. It's great fun!

6 I don't like watching **romantic / horror** films before I go to sleep because they give me scary dreams.

2 Read the clues and complete the crossword.

Down
1 someone who performs comedy
2 someone who plays music
3 someone who does magic tricks
4 someone who acts

Across
5 someone who plays the guitar
6 someone who sings
7 someone who dances

3 🔊 5.4 Listen and complete the sentences with the adjectives you hear.

1 We saw a .... film at the weekend. We left half way through it!

2 Rachel is an .... musician. She's the best guitarist I know!

3 The comedian was wearing a .... shirt with elephants all over it!

4 I saw a really .... horror film at the weekend. I couldn't sleep afterwards!

5 It was really .... of you to buy me a cinema ticket.

6 This action film is .... It's full of surprises and has great actors in it!

4 e Read the blog post. Choose the correct answer for each gap.

Walkley talent show

Last night Walkley High School had its first <u>talent show</u> . I arrived at school at 7 p.m. Students were getting ready for the show. It felt very **1** .... Twenty-five students were **2** .... part in total. The show started at 7.30 p.m. with some **3** .... They were playing a pop song. After that, we saw comedians, dancers and even a magician! At nine o'clock the teachers chose the best **4** .... Then the headteacher read the name of the winner. It was Jack Hill! But Jack was so surprised he didn't move from his **5** .... ! All of Jack's friends started shouting his name and he got up and collected his prize. He was laughing with everyone else! It was so funny! We're all looking forward to next year's show!

	A animation	**B** talent show	**C** music festival
1	**A** exciting	**B** awesome	**C** afraid
2	**A** playing	**B** acting	**C** taking
3	**A** musicians	**B** actors	**C** players
4	**A** exhibition	**B** act	**C** show
5	**A** armchair	**B** desk	**C** seat

Extend

5 Complete the questions with these words.

author   go out   news   opera   sad   star

1 Where do you .... with your friends at the weekend?
2 Who is the .... of your favourite book?
3 Do you know someone who likes .... and pop music?
4 Who is the most popular film .... in your country?
5 Do you like to read the .... about your favourite bands or singers online?
6 Do you prefer .... or funny films?

LISTENING

1 e 🔊 5.5 **Listen and for each question, choose the correct picture.**

1 How much is a small drink in the cinema?

 (A)  (B)   (C)

2 Who did Anna go to the theatre with?

(A)   (B)   (C)

3 What time does the art exhibition open?

 A 9:45  B 10:20   C 10:30

4 What is Barney learning to do?

(A)   (B)  (C)

5 Where is Katya watching the horror film?

 A  B  C

2 🔊 5.6 **Listen again and answer the questions.**

1 What drink does the boy choose in the cinema?

....

2 What is the relationship between Anna and Jackie?

....

3 Who did Anna and Jackie see at the theatre?

....

4 What is special about the art exhibition that Aaron's going to?

....

5 Does Barney know how to play the guitar?

....

6 Why didn't Katya watch the film in the lounge?

....

past continuous and past simple

3 **Match 1–6 with A–F to make sentences.**

1 My friend sent me a message ....
2 When Tom was buying drinks, ...
3 The comedian tried his best, ...
4 Florence and Jo were looking at a Picasso painting ....
5 When we arrived at the concert, ...
6 They didn't go to the open-air theatre because ....

A but no one was laughing at his jokes.
B the band was already playing the first song.
C when I was watching a documentary.
D when we saw them at the art exhibition.
E it was raining and cold.
F Marcus found seats for them.

4 **Complete the sentences with the past simple or past continuous form of the verbs in brackets.**

1 She .... (watch) an action film when she .... (hear) the loud noise outside.
2 Kieran and Joe .... (find) an old violin when they .... (look) in their grandpa's cupboard.
3 I .... (stand) outside the theatre when I .... (see) my favourite actor.
4 The tour guide .... (tell) us about the famous paintings when my phone .... (ring).
5 Alice .... (dance) when she .... (hurt) her leg.
6 They .... (have) dinner when they .... (hear) the news.

5 **Complete the text with the correct form of these verbs.**

be   change   drive   get   love   not look forward to

Yesterday when my dad ¹......................... me home from school, he said he had a surprise for me. I was very excited. I was thinking the surprise was maybe a pizza for dinner or a film at the cinema. I ²......................... wrong. The surprise was tickets for a concert. I was hoping it was a band I liked or at least knew! When I ³......................... ready for the concert, Dad showed me the tickets. It was a classical music concert! Suddenly, I wasn't excited anymore. I ⁴......................... an evening of classical music! But we went and I ⁵......................... it! I was wrong about classical music. After the concert, I ⁶......................... my opinion. It was a brilliant experience!

43

SPEAKING

1 Choose the correct words to complete the sentences.

1 I prefer **watch / watching** films at the cinema.
2 I **'m preferring / prefer** concerts because I love live music.
3 I don't really enjoy **going / to go** to sports events.
4 I **enjoy / 'm enjoying** art exhibitions.
5 I **'m thinking / think** art exhibitions are a bit boring.
6 I don't like **going / go** to comedy shows.

2 🔊 5.7 **Listen to a conversation. Which of these types of entertainment do the speakers talk about?**

art exhibitions   comedy shows   dance shows   festivals   films
magic shows   sports events   talent shows

3 🔊 5.8 **Listen again and complete the conversation.**

What do you think about art exhibitions, Josh? Do you like them?

I like some art exhibitions, but I ¹.......................... to sports events like football matches. How about you?

I love art, so I ².......................... art exhibitions. I ³.......................... watching football, but I enjoy other sports like tennis or basketball.

Do you like going to the theatre? I think ⁴.......................... .

I don't. I really enjoy the theatre. I like watching comedy shows or dance shows.

Yes, I enjoy comedy shows, too. I like watching bands at the theatre, but I ⁵.......................... music at festivals. I think festivals are more fun.

I agree. You can dance and walk around. I ⁶.......................... in a theatre listening to music.

4 🔊 5.9 **Listen and complete the questions.**

1 What .... you .... when you .... this morning?
2 What .... your friends .... when you .... at school today?
3 What .... you .... about when you .... dinner yesterday?
4 What .... you .... when you .... your last text message?
5 Where .... you .... when you .... last in a car?
6 .... it .... when you .... your house this morning?

5 Answer the questions in Ex 4.

1 ....
2 ....
3 ....
4 ....
5 ....
6 ....

WRITING

1 Put the sentences in the correct order (1–5) to make a story.

A We were trying on trainers when a dog ran into the shop. ....

B A few seconds later we heard the dog's owner: 'Ruby! Come here!' He was the loudest person in the shop. ....

C At the end of it all, the shop assistants were all laughing. I was glad he found his dog! ....

D Last weekend I was shopping with my friends at our favourite sports shop called Spark. ....

E Then the dog picked up a tennis racket and brought it to his owner. ....

2 Complete the blog post. Write one word for each gap.

Hi, I'm Felicity. My family and I love going ¹........................... the market at the weekend. ²........................... sells food, sunglasses and clothing. We often eat unusual (but delicious!) food from all over the world. The ³........................... thing is that the prices are good. The worst thing ⁴........................... that it's always busy. Last Saturday I found a hoodie for five euros. It was a ⁵........................... .

3 Complete the sentences with the correct form of the verbs in brackets.

A I ¹........................... (know) the song really well, but no sounds were coming out of my mouth. I couldn't remember any of the words! It was terrible. It felt like I ²........................... (stand) there for hours!

B I was the first act in the talent show. As I ³........................... (walk) onto the stage, I saw the school hall was full of students, parents and teachers.

C I was starting to feel sick and I ⁴........................... (want) to run off the stage. Then I heard the words, 'Time to wake up!' It was a just a dream – thankfully!

D A few seconds later, the band ⁵........................... (start) playing my song and everyone was looking at me. They ⁶........................... (wait) for me to sing.

4 Put the paragraphs in Ex 3 in the correct order (1–4) to make a story.

1 ....   **2** ....   **3** ....   **4** ....

5 Look at the three pictures. Write the story shown in the pictures. Write 35 words or more.

UNIT CHECK

1 Complete the sentences with these words.

funny hurry laptop nice practice thirsty

1 I'm really ....! Can we get a drink?
2 We watched a really .... comedian.
3 It takes an hour to get there. .... up!
4 And wear something ....!
5 My teacher gave me some .... exercises to do.
6 She's watching the film on the ....

2 Complete the sentences with the past continuous form of these verbs.

listen not sleep not watch sing talk wear

1 Why .... Nick .... that funny hat?
2 My parents .... to classical music last night.
3 We .... a romantic film yesterday. It was a horror film.
4 Who .... you .... to yesterday morning?
5 I .... I was reading my book in bed.
6 The teachers .... a song in the show.

3 Choose the correct words to complete the sentences.

1 They **watched / were watching** a comedy on TV when we **got / were getting** back from the party.
2 Robbie **played / was playing** football when he **broke / was breaking** his arm.
3 They **saw / were seeing** the film star when they **bought / were buying** their theatre tickets.
4 I **didn't listen / wasn't listening** when my guitar teacher **gave / was giving** me my homework.
5 When they **arrived / were arriving** at the cinema, Harriet **ate / was eating** a big bag of popcorn.
6 They **waited / were waiting** outside the art exhibition when it **started / was starting** to rain.
7 Lisa **lost / was losing** her ring while she **swam / was swimming**.
8 It **rained / was raining** when I **got up / was getting up** this morning.

4 Make sentences. Use the past simple and past continuous.

1 we / sit / in a London café / when / we / see / my favourite singer

....

2 I / watch / a documentary / when / I / fall / asleep

....

3 Emma / listen / to music / when / you / call / her

....

4 I / meet / my best friend / when / I / perform / in a talent show

....

5 we / visit / an art exhibition / when / I / get / your message

....

6 I / wait / outside the festival / when / I / send / Tom a message

....

5 Complete the conversation with the past simple or past continuous form of the verbs in brackets.

A: What **1** .... you .... (do) after school today? I **2** .... (not see) you at drama club.
B: I couldn't go today. I **3** .... (need) some new dance shoes for the dance show on Saturday.
A: **4** .... you .... (get) some?
B: Yes, but we **5** .... (look) for ages before we found some. I missed drama club. What did you do?
A: For most of the time we **6** .... (practise) for the show. Freddie got into trouble with the drama teacher!
B: Really? **7** .... he .... (talk) too much again?
A: No, he **8** .... (play) games on his phone! Miss King **9** .... (not be) happy!

REVIEW: UNITS 1–5

1 Choose the correct answer, A, B or C.

1 Do you go to this festival every year?

  A Yes, I do.

  B Yes, I am.

  C Yes, I go.

2 What's Mark doing in the other room?

  A He's in the living room.

  B He watches TV with his brother.

  C He's chatting online with friends.

3 Where did you buy that notebook?

  A It's in my bag.

  B I write my homework in it.

  C At the supermarket.

4 What were you doing at 10 p.m. last night?

  A I'm studying for an exam.

  B Nothing. I was asleep.

  C I talked to my dad.

5 How much is this tablet?

  A Yes, it's too much.

  B It costs money.

  C It's £149.

6 Why did you buy these trainers?

  A They were the cheapest.

  B Trainers are cheap.

  C They're my new trainers.

7 Can we pay by card?

  A Yes, but in cash.

  B Yes, I think we can.

  C Yes, they only take cash.

2 Complete the sentences with these words.

after	at	because	but	end	that

1 My maths homework was really hard. In the
............................, I called my friend for help.

2 I spoke to Ed on the phone yesterday, ...
I didn't see him.

3 I bought a new phone last Wednesday ....
I broke my old one.

4 I had a science lesson .... lunch.

5 Layla was feeling really tired .... the end of
the day.

6 I had my guitar lesson and after .... I met
my friend.

3 Complete the review with these words.

comedian	enjoy	marks	prefer	talent show	take part

The **Great Cooking Show**

I love 'The Great Cooking Show'. It's like a **1**............................
for teenage cooks. Ten teenagers **2**............................ in the
show and every week they have to cook different things.
They do the cooking in a TV studio. At the end of the
show they get **3**............................ for their cooking. There are
four judges who give marks. Three of them are famous
chefs, but one judge is a **4**............................ .
She's really funny. I really **5**............................
cooking, but I wouldn't like to be
on 'The Great Cooking Show'.
I **6**............................ watching it from my
home. It's my favourite
programme on TV!

4 Complete the conversation. Write one word for each gap.

A: Hurry **1**............................, Yasmin! The film **2**............................
starting.

B: I'm coming! I **3**............................ just getting some
popcorn from the kitchen.

A: Great! Can I have some too, please?

B: Yes, here you **4**............................ . This doesn't look like a
science fiction film. It looks like a romantic comedy.
Are you sure it's the right one?

A: Yes, I **5**............................ . Look at the TV magazine – nine
o'clock, Channel 3, 'The Day of the Aliens'.

B: Yes, Oliver, but you're **6**............................ at the page for
Saturday. It's Friday today!

A: Oh no! I **7**............................ looking forward to that film.
And I hate romantic films!

B: I **8**............................ . I love them. Bad luck!

47

Are we there yet?

READING

1 Match sentences 1–6 with sentences A–F.

1 My uncle is Welsh. ....
2 We go to Italy twice a year. ....
3 We saw lots of camels on holiday in Morocco. ....
4 My sister's a big football fan. ....
5 This chair is very comfortable. ....
6 This is a high-speed train. ....

A They're my favourite animals.
B It's got big soft cushions on it.
C Once in the summer and once in January.
D He comes from Cardiff in Wales.
E It travels much faster than the normal ones.
F She loves watching Manchester United play.

2 Read the article. Which of these places in Hong Kong does Amy write about?

Nan Lian Garden   Nathan Road   Ocean Park
Victoria Harbour   Victoria Peak

3 e Read the article again. For each question, choose the correct answer.

1 Amy knows Hong Kong well because
  A she lives there with her family.
  B she went there on holiday a lot when she was young.
  C she lived there until she was a teenager.

2 Why does Amy think Hong Kong is a great place for teenagers?
  A because it's easy to get bored in other cities
  B because there are many things to interest teenagers
  C because there are so many young people there

3 Amy thinks the best way to see the city is
  A by boat.   B on foot.   C by tram.

4 Amy says Victoria Peak
  A is a beautiful place to stay for a night.
  B has great views in the evening.
  C has no restaurants or cafes.

5 Amy sometimes feels that Nathan Road is
  A too expensive.   B too long.   C too busy.

Visiting Hong Kong?
Here's what you need to know

In this month's "Teen Travels" we talk to Amy Lee about advice for teenage visitors to Hong Kong.

So, Amy, why is Hong Kong a cool place for teens to visit?

It's the best city, in my opinion. I now live in London, but I spent the first twelve years of my life in Hong Kong. I go back to Hong Kong every holiday to visit family. In fact, I'm going to be there next week. For me, it's a really exciting city to be in and there is so much for young people to do. You'll never get bored in Hong Kong!

I like walking around Hong Kong and also catching the tram, but my favourite way to see the city is from the water. You can catch the Star Ferry from Victoria Harbour. You'll get amazing views of Hong Kong and it's not an expensive way to travel. I also love going up to Victoria Peak, the highest mountain on Hong Kong Island. You can take a tram up the mountain. There are places to eat, but no hotels. It's especially good at nighttime, when you can see all the lights of Hong Kong below you.

A favourite place for Hong Kong teens to walk along is Nathan Road. It's two miles long and is full of shops, but also full of people – sometimes too many! The bubble tea shops are really popular places for teens to hang out. You'll have no problem spending your holiday money there!

I hope you have a great time in Hong Kong!

GRAMMAR

talking about the future

1 Make questions with *going to*.

1 you / travel / to Morocco / by plane?

....

2 we / stay / for seven nights?

....

3 she / stay / with a family in Brazil?

....

4 what / you / do / next summer?

....

5 when / she / learn to drive?

....

2 Complete Harriet's plans for the weekend. Use *going to* and the verbs in brackets.

My friend Francesca ¹.. (spend)
this weekend with me. I ²..
(meet) her on Saturday morning at the train station
and we ³.. (walk) to the
shopping centre. She wants to buy a new coat, but
I ⁴.. (not buy) anything. In
the evening we ⁵.. (see) some
other friends and watch a film together. Francesca
⁶.. (stay) the night at my house.
On Sunday we ⁷.. (not do)
anything — just relax!

3 Complete the sentences with *will* or *won't* and these verbs.

be   buy   catch   leave   take

1 Tom's mum usually drives him home from school, but today I think he .... the bus.

2 Next year I think my uncle .... us to the South of France.

3 Kirsty .... late for dinner because she missed her bus.

4 Liam's parents .... him a motorbike. They think motorbikes are dangerous.

5 The ferry .... on time because of the bad weather.

4 🔊 6.1 Listen and complete the conversation.

A: Hi, Penny. Where ¹........................ you .... the school holidays?

B: Hi, Charlie. I ²........................ probably .... with my grandparents as usual. How about you?

A: I ³........................ at football camp for two weeks. I can't wait!

B: You'll love that! Are you going to sleep at the camp too?

A: Yes, it's in London, so I ⁴........................ the train there. My brother's going to come with me, so we'll travel together.

B: Sounds like it's going to be fun. So when you come back, you ⁵........................ the best footballer at school!

A: I'm not sure that ⁶........................ ! But hopefully, I'm going to get better.

5 Match the questions (1–6) with the answers (A–F).

1 Will they miss the train? ....

2 Is she going to catch the nine o'clock bus? ....

3 Are they going to fly to Greece? ....

4 Will you meet me on the platform? ....

5 Are you going to go on foot? ....

6 Will Alice wait for George at the port? ....

A Yes, they are.   **D** Yes, I will.

B No, I'm not.   **E** Yes, she will.

C No, they won't.   **F** No, she isn't.

6 🔊 6.2 Listen and repeat the questions and answers in Ex 5.

7 🔊 6.3 Listen, speak and record. Listen back and compare.

VOCABULARY

transport

1 Choose the correct words to complete the conversations.

1 A: Do you walk to school?

B: No, I take the school **bus / underground**.

2 A: Is your brother on a school trip?

B: Yes. He's in Switzerland. They're on a **coach / ferry** trip through the mountains.

3 A: How do you travel between the islands?

B: There's a small **ship / ferry**. It carries about thirty passengers.

4 A: What did you do for your birthday?

B: My uncle took me on a **helicopter / motorbike** ride. It was my first time flying.

5 A: How long does it take you to travel to Moscow?

B: Five hours. We usually go by **tram / train**.

6 A: What's the best way to get to the library?

B: Take the **tram / coach** because the traffic is always bad in the city centre.

2 Complete the sentences with these words.

catch   drive   fly   ride   sail   travel

1 We usually .... by plane when we visit my aunty in France.

2 Every morning the fishermen .... out to sea in their fishing boats.

3 My uncle and dad have the same job. They both .... a taxi.

4 I'd like to learn to .... a helicopter.

5 Can your brother .... a motorbike?

6 We don't live near school, so we .... the school bus every day.

3 Match the pictures (1–6) with these places.

airport   bus stop   car park   coach station   platform   port

4 🔊 6.4 Complete the text. Write one word for each gap. Listen and check your answers.

Hi! My name's Olivia and I live on an island. The island's not big and there are no buses or [1]..........................., so I usually go everywhere on [2]........................... . My parents both [3]..........................., but they sold their car when we moved to the island. Every month we go to the city on the mainland. First we take the [4]........................... from the harbour and then we [5]........................... the train to the city centre. I really enjoy the [6]........................... . There's a famous businessman who lives on my island. I know he has a [7]........................... and flies to the mainland. I think that's a really cool way to travel!

Extend

5 Choose the correct words to complete the sentences.

1 Excuse me, does the bus **stop / pause** here?

2 I'm sorry I'm late, but the bad weather **held / delayed** our train.

3 The best way to **learn / explore** this city is on foot.

4 We were late for dinner because we **missed / lost** our train.

5 It's better to catch the bus into town because there's nowhere to **park / stop** your car.

6 We walked to the cinema, but we **finished / returned** home by taxi.

50

LISTENING

1 🔊 6.5 **Listen to Jack and Melissa. What are they talking about?**

2 ℮ 🔊 6.6 **Listen again and for each question, choose the correct answer. What type of transport is each person going to use on Saturday?**

People		Types of transport
Alex	..E..	**A** bike
1 Melissa	....	**B** bus
2 Lily	....	**C** train
3 Ewan	....	**D** underground
4 Henry	....	**E** ferry
5 Emma	....	**F** plane
		G car
		H motorbike

3 🔊 6.7 **Listen again. Are the sentences true (T) or false (F)?**

1 Melissa and Jack are cousins. ....
2 Alex is going to travel alone. ....
3 Melissa will eat before she goes to Jack's house on Saturday. ....
4 Jack's parents are going to help him prepare for the party. ....
5 Ewan lives with his uncle. ....
6 Emma's brother is going to go out on Saturday night. ....

present continuous for future

4 **Complete the sentences. Use the present continuous form of the verbs in brackets.**

1 Here are your tickets. The ferry ....'s leaving.... (leave) in ten minutes.
2 Rachel .... (not come) on the trip tomorrow. She's not very well.
3 Here's a picture of our new car. Mum .... (collect) it from the garage next week.
4 I can't come with you to the café. I .... (meet) my cousins at the train station in five minutes.
5 Simon .... (not see) Will and Suzie this evening. He's got too much homework to do.

5 🔊 6.8 **Listen and answer the questions.**

1 Where's Oliver going on holiday?
....
2 When's he going?
....
3 How's he getting there?
....
4 How long is he going for?
....
5 Where's he staying?
....
6 Who's he going with?
....

6 **Complete the text. Write one word for each gap.**

Class 9B school trip to Paris

This year we're **1**.................... to Paris for our school trip. We're staying in Paris **2**.................... two nights. We're travelling to the port of Dover **3**.................... coach and catching a ferry to France. Then we **4**.................... travelling by coach to Paris. We're **5**.................... in a hotel in the centre of the city. I **6**.................... having a meeting next Tuesday evening at 6.30 p.m. to discuss the trip with all students and parents.

Mr Evans
Year 9 French teacher

SPEAKING

1 Complete the sentences with these verbs.

'm going out	'm having	'm walking	're learning
	's flying	is going	

1 My dad .... to Japan tomorrow morning.
2 I .... home after school today.
3 We .... to speak Chinese next year.
4 I .... with my friends this evening.
5 I .... lunch at school tomorrow.
6 My class .... on a school trip this year.

2 Put the words in the correct order to make questions.

1 are / going to / see / in the holidays / who / you?

....

2 you / what / going to / are / do?

....

3 in Lisbon / it / be / will / hot?

....

4 next week / you / going / to Italy / are?

....

5 is / it / cost / going to / how much?

....

6 you / are / when /going / to Turkey?

....

3 Make present continuous questions.

1 where / you / go / on holiday / this summer?

....

2 when / you / go?

....

3 how / you / get / there?

....

4 how long / you / go for?

....

5 where / you / stay?

....

6 who / you / go with?

....

4 Choose the correct words to complete the conversation.

A: What are you **¹going to / will** do in the summer, Poppy?

B: I'm going to Australia. How **²about / for** you?

A: I'm going to go camping with my sister. Where **³are / will** you going to stay in Australia?

B: With my grandparents, in Sydney.

A: That **⁴'s sounding / sounds** great! Will it be hot?

B: Not really, probably about seventeen degrees. It will be winter in Australia.

A: When are you **⁵leaving / leave**?

B: We're flying next Monday.

A: Lucky you! **⁶Have / Do** a good trip!

B: Thanks!

5 🔊 6.9 **Listen and repeat.**

1 I'm going to Spain. How about you?
2 I'm going to New York.
3 Lucky you! Have a good trip!

6 🔊 6.10 **Listen, speak and record. Listen back and compare.**

WRITING

1 Complete the sentences with *at, by, in, on* or *to*.

1 We're travelling to France .... train.
2 Emma and her friends are planning a trip .... Italy.
3 He's catching the ferry .... ten o'clock.
4 I'm going to go .... foot. ot the football stadium.
5 She's going to sit .... this seat and look out the window.

2 Match the questions (1–5) with the answers (A–E).

1 Are they going to dinner tonight?
2 Will you take your headphones?
3 Is she catching the train home?
4 Will it be warm in Spain?
5 Is he going to buy a new T-shirt?

A Yes, it will.
B Yes, he is.
C No, I won't.
D Yes, they are.
E No, she isn't.

3 Put the sentences from Carlos's email (A–F) to Heidi in the correct order (1–6).

A Guess what! I'm going to Russia with my school. We're flying to Moscow on Thursday. Then we're taking a train to St Petersburg. ....
B Hi Heidi, ...
C Carlos ....
D I'll take lots of photos to show you. ....
E Bye for now. ....
F I'm looking forward to seeing the palaces and going on a boat trip! ....

4 Complete the email with these words.

at   in   journey   on   to   trip

To: Isaac
From: Marinella
Subject: Trip to Mount Olympus

Hi Isaac,

Did you get my text? I'm going on a school ¹ .... at the weekend. We're leaving on Saturday and travelling by plane ² .... Athens. Then we're catching a coach to Mount Olympus ³ .... six o'clock the next morning! The ⁴ .... will take about six hours!

Mount Olympus is the highest mountain ⁵ .... Greece. We're going to climb to the top. We're staying in a hotel in a small town called Litochoro. We're coming back ⁶ .... Monday. It will be amazing!

5 Read the email in Ex 4 again and complete the notes.

Duration of trip: ¹ ....
Types of transport: ² ...., ³ ....
Time to leave for Mount Olympus: ⁴ ....
Hotel location: ⁵ ....
Return day: ⁶ ....

6 **e** You are going on holiday with your family. Write an email to your friend. Write where and when you are going and what you are going to do there. Remember to start and finish in a friendly way. Write 25 words or more.

UNIT CHECK

1 Match the words in bold in the sentences (1–6) with their meanings (A–F).

1 We took a **high-speed** train from Tokyo to Kyoto. ......

2 How much is a train **ticket** to Istanbul? ......

3 The school is organising a weekend **trip** to Madrid. ......

4 I always get bored on a long **journey**. ......

5 It's a four-hour **flight** to Warsaw. I hope I have a window seat on the plane! ......

6 Can all **passengers** travelling to Gloucester please get off the train now? ......

A the act of travelling from one place to another

B a person who is using a kind of transport but is not driving it, flying it or sailing it

C when you go somewhere, usually for a short time, and come back again

D a journey in a plane

E very fast

F a small piece of paper or card to show you paid for a journey

2 Complete the table with these words.

~~bike~~ coach ferry helicopter motorbike plane ship
train tram underground

land	air	sea
bike		

3 Complete the questions with *will* and these verbs. Complete the short answers with *will* or *won't*.

bring buy miss phone send take

1 A: .... you .... me an email?
   B: Yes, I ....

2 A: .... she .... a lot of luggage with her when she comes?
   B: No, she ....

3 A: .... they .... their friends and family?
   B: Yes, they ....

4 A: .... we .... our tickets before we go?
   B: No, we ....

5 A: .... he .... lots of photos with his new camera?
   B: Yes, he ....

6 A: .... you .... me tomorrow evening from your hotel room?
   B: Yes, I ....

4 Complete the conversation. Write one word for each gap.

A: Hurry up! The train ¹........................... leaving in twenty minutes and it ²........................... take us fifteen minutes to walk to the station.

B: OK! ³........................... you taking your sunglasses with you?

A: Yes, it's ⁴........................... to be hot and sunny today.

B: Oh, great! I ⁵........................... bring some sun cream, too. Are we going ⁶........................... have a picnic at the castle?

A: No, we'll buy lunch at the café there.

B: How ⁷........................... we get from the station to the castle?

A: On foot – it's not far. Anyway, we ⁸........................... going to be late, come on.

B: All right. I'm ready!

REVIEW: UNITS 1–6

1 **Where are they? Match the conversations (1–6) with these places.**

changing room   department store   kitchen   library
port   theatre

1 A: Excuse me, could you bring me this dress in a larger size, please?

B: Yes, of course. Is that a small or medium?

....

2 A: Can we do some baking, Dad?

B: Yes, sure. We can make some biscuits. Can you get the butter from the fridge?

....

3 A: Excuse me, do you know which is the ferry to Dover?

B: Yes, it's the large boat over there called The Sea Star.

....

4 A: Do you have this book by Arthur Grant?

B: Let me have a look. Yes, we do. You'll find it over there on the first bookshelf.

....

5 A: Hello. Where can I find shoes?

B: Shoes and bags are on the second floor next to men's clothes.

....

6 A: We're going to be late; the show will start soon. It's 7.30!

B: Don't worry, here are our seats – J17 and J18. Just in time!

....

2 **Complete the sentences. Write one word for each gap.**

1 Beth loves listening .... music on her phone.

2 It's easy to buy tickets from this website. You just need to click .... this link.

3 In my classroom, Anna sits behind me and Jack sits in .... of me.

4 My mum paid .... my new trainers. It was a birthday present.

5 'Avatar' is my favourite science .... film.

6 We don't have our chemistry lesson in a normal classroom. We have it in the science ....

3 **Choose the correct answer, A, B or C.**

1 I think it's very .... of comedians to tell jokes in front of so many people.

A great   **B** boring   **C** brave

2 We went on an awesome day .... to Shell Island.

A trip   **B** journey   **C** travel

3 It's a good idea to .... clothes before you buy them.

A get on   **B** try on   **C** go out

4 We're .... a history exam next Tuesday.

A writing   **B** answering   **C** having

5 I enjoy .... music in the evening after I finish my homework.

A riding   **B** streaming   **C** looking

6 Ben won a fishing .... last week. The prize was £50!

A competition   **B** festival   **C** show

4 **e** **Read the email. Choose the correct answer for each gap.**

Hi Jane,

I'm so excited! We're going to visit my cousins in Australia next week. We're going to take a coach to Heathrow Airport. Then we're ¹........................... a plane to Singapore. We'll stay there for a few days and then we'll take another plane to Australia. We're arriving in Sydney late ²........................... night. My uncle's meeting us at the airport and he'll drive us to his house in Newcastle. My uncle's got a boat and he says he'll teach me to ³...........................! My uncle's got three children – two boys and a girl. They're all older ⁴........................... me, but we always have fun together. My oldest cousin's got a motorbike. It's really cool and it ⁵........................... a lot of money. I really want to go on it. I hope he says I can!

Speak soon,
Adam

	A go	**B** travel	**C** take
1	**A** catching	**B** flying	**C** riding
2	**A** in	**B** at	**C** of
3	**A** sail	**B** ride	**C** drive
4	**A** to	**B** from	**C** than
5	**A** spent	**B** cost	**C** paid

READING

1 **Complete the sentences with these words.**

> coach   course   referee   reporter   skills
> sports journalism

1 The .... gave the football player a red card because he kicked another player.

2 Eddie loves writing about sport. He'd like a job in .... in the future.

3 My dad's a basketball .... He teaches our town's basketball team.

4 Sports teach important .... such as teamwork.

5 A .... from the local newspaper interviewed the winners of the race.

6 My cousin's doing a .... in sports science at university.

2 **Read the article quickly. Choose the correct answer.**

The idea of the MyMiles challenge is to

A test how many miles you can walk, cycle or swim in seven days.

B get people to do more exercise and help future sports stars.

C get lazy people to exercise more often and have a healthier life.

A good reason to get moving!

The #MyMiles challenge invites **1**........ of all ages to do some exercise and collect money to help young sportspeople. The idea is to do one mile – or forty miles of exercise **2**........ one week. You can complete your mile in different ways. You can walk to school, cycle or **3**........ for a swim. Twenty minutes of dancing or judo also count as one mile. The number of miles you do is not important – it's **4**........ part that matters. After you do your mile or miles, **5**........ a video or photo on social media. Then ask a friend to do the same as you. Don't forget to give £2 when you finish. All the money from #MyMiles helps young sports stars with training and competition **6**........ .

3 **e** **Read the article again. For each question, choose the correct answer for each gap.**

1 **A** someone   **B** people   **C** anyone

2 **A** in   **B** on   **C** at

3 **A** do   **B** go   **C** make

4 **A** making   **B** getting   **C** taking

5 **A** share   **B** give   **C** open

6 **A** prices   **B** costs   **C** sales

4 **Read Damien's comment about the challenge and answer the questions.**

1 What does Damien like about the challenge?

....

2 What sport does a member of his family do?

....

3 Why doesn't he do team sports like football?

....

4 Who did he do the MyMiles challenge with?

....

5 What surprised him about the video?

....

6 Who is going to do the MyMiles challenge next?

....

Doing the #MyMiles challenge!

Damien

Hi, my name's Damien and I did the #MyMiles challenge. I think it's a great idea because you can do any kind of exercise you like. My brother's crazy about running, but I find it boring. I also don't really enjoy team sports like football. It's not because I can't play – I'm actually quite good. So when I heard about #MyMiles, I wanted to think of a different kind of exercise. I decided to choose something I love doing: skateboarding. I did it with a group of school friends. My sister took a video of us while we were skateboarding. We can do lots of different jumps. I uploaded the video to my social media page. And amazingly, hundreds of people liked the video. I enjoyed showing my friends what I can do on my skateboard. I had some really cool comments from people. I gave my £2 and I think my whole school made about £500 in total to help young sportspeople. I'm going to get my dad to do the #MyMiles challenge now – that will be fun!

GRAMMAR

ability: *can/could*

1 Complete the sentences. Use *can* or *can't* and the verbs in brackets.

1 Ruby .... (swim). She's afraid of water.

2 My parents .... (ride) a bike. They go cycling in the mountains.

3 Mark and Karen .... (surf). They take their boards to the beach every weekend.

4 I .... (skateboard). I tried it once, but I fell off all the time. I didn't enjoy it.

5 Lily .... (run) very fast. She won a competition last month.

2 Make questions with *can*. Then complete the short answers.

1 Mark / play / volleyball?
A: ....
B: Yes, ...

2 you / do / gymnastics?
A: ....
B: No, ...

3 your sister / ski?
A: ....
B: Yes, ...

4 Amelia and Eve / swim?
A: ....
B: Yes, ...

5 Max / ride / bike?
A: ....
B: No, ...

6 your cousins / play / volleyball?
A: ....
B: No, ...

3 Read the sentences. Are they about ability (A) or possibility (P)?

1 Emilia can run 5 km in thirty-five minutes. ....

2 The swimming pool can get very busy on Saturdays. ....

3 Anyone can learn to play tennis – it just takes a lot of practice. ....

4 It can't be time to leave the pool – we only just arrived! ....

5 Sophie couldn't cycle as fast as her sister. ....

4 🔊 7.1 Listen to three conversations. Complete them with *can*, *can't*, *could* or *couldn't*.

1 A: I remember the first time I went surfing. I **1**.......................... stay on the board! **2**.......................... you surf?
B: Yes, I **3**.......................... . I go surfing with my brothers in the summer.

2 A: **4**.......................... you play tennis when you were five?
B: No, I **5**.........................., but I learnt to play when I was seven.

3 A: **6**.......................... you ski, Max?
B: No, I **7**.........................., but I'm going for the first time this December. I **8**.......................... skateboard so I think it will be easy to learn.

5 Put the words in the correct order to make sentences. Which sentences are true for you?

1 'hello' / can / different languages / say / I / in eight
....

2 play / can / well / basketball / my dad / really
....

3 when / couldn't / I / swim / five years old / was / I
....

4 went / I / the last time / I / swimming / remember / can't
....

5 can / in winter / it / snow / in my country
....

57

VOCABULARY

sport

1 Complete the advert with the correct words.

White Beach Activity Centre

We have an activity for everyone here at White Beach!

For people who like water sports, we have

.....surfing..... and **1** ....

for all levels and ages. There are also lots of team

games such as football and **2** ....

Our outdoor activities include **3** ....

and **4** ....

When the weather is bad, we have great indoor

activities to offer. Why not try **5** .... or

6 .... ? Our teachers are friendly

and helpful.

We hope to see you at White Beach soon!

2 Complete the sentences with *practice* or the correct form of *practise*.

1 All great tennis players .... a lot.

2 We have hockey .... in the school field at 3.30 p.m.

3 Danny did lots of ...., but he still didn't win the match.

4 I .... diving every day of the holiday until I became really good.

5 Tom will never be in the gymnastics team because he .... enough.

6 Rebecca didn't go to badminton .... because she wasn't feeling very well.

3 Choose the correct answer, A, B or C.

1 Why have you got that racket with you?
  A I've got a tennis lesson after school.
  B I'm playing in a basketball match later.
  C I'm going swimming with my sister.

2 Have you got any goggles I can borrow?
  A No, sorry. I don't play football.
  B Yes, I'll bring them to the swimming pool.
  C Yes, I have to wear them for gymnastics.

3 Isn't it a bit cold for surfing today, Jane?
  A Don't worry, I'll wear goggles.
  B Don't worry, I'll wear a swimsuit.
  C Don't worry, I'll wear a wetsuit.

4 Why can't we play volleyball today?
  A The board's broken.
  B The net's broken.
  C The helmet's broken.

5 Is that a new board, Gina?
  A Yes, I'm going to the gym now.
  B Yes, I'm going to the swimming pool now.
  C Yes, I'm going to the skateboarding park now.

6 Can I go horse-riding with Ella, Mum?
  A OK, but don't forget your helmet.
  B OK, but don't forget your ball.
  C OK, but don't forget your net.

Extend

4 🔊 7.2 **Listen and match the speakers (1–6) with these sports.**

baseball	cricket	golf	rugby	volleyball	windsurfing

1 ....   **4** ....
2 ....   **5** ....
3 ....   **6** ....

LISTENING

1 🔊 **7.3 Listen to five conversations. Which sports from A and which equipment from B do you hear?**

A badminton basketball cycling diving football
gymnastics hockey judo running surfing
swimming tennis

B board goggles helmet net racket swimsuit
trainers wetsuit

2 🄴 🔊 **7.4 Listen again. For each question, choose the correct picture.**

1 What is Lara learning to do at the moment?

2 Where is Jess' football shirt?

3 What time does gymnastics club start?

4 What did Rob get for his birthday?

5 How much were Matt's goggles?

3 🔊 **7.5 Listen again and complete the sentences.**

1 Alice is going to teach Lara to ....

2 Jess needs her shirt because she's got football ....

3 Ann and Jo are going to meet .... the gym.

4 Isaac's going to show Rob his .... next time they play tennis together.

5 Matt didn't buy his goggles in a shop. He bought them ....

obligation: *have to/had to*

4 **Complete the sentences with these phrases.**

doesn't have to don't have to has to have to (x2)

1 Rebecca .... wear a helmet when she goes horse-riding.

2 You .... wear goggles when you go skiing, but it's a good idea.

3 Sometimes they .... finish tennis matches early because of rain.

4 Ella .... do gymnastics at school, but she chooses to do it.

5 Mathew and Clara .... cycle to school because their mum doesn't have a car.

5 🔊 **7.6 Listen and repeat.**

1 Do you have to do sport at your school?

2 Do you have to walk to school every day?

3 When did you last have to wear trainers?

4 When was the last time you had to run really fast?

6 🔊 **7.7 Listen, speak and record. Listen back and compare.**

7 **Complete the text. Write one word for each gap.**

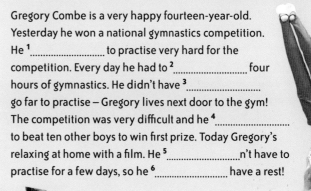

Local boy number *1* in gymnastics competition!

Gregory Combe is a very happy fourteen-year-old. Yesterday he won a national gymnastics competition. He **1** .... to practise very hard for the competition. Every day he had to **2** .... four hours of gymnastics. He didn't have **3** .... go far to practise – Gregory lives next door to the gym! The competition was very difficult and he **4** .... to beat ten other boys to win first prize. Today Gregory's relaxing at home with a film. He **5** ....n't have to practise for a few days, so he **6** .... have a rest!

SPEAKING

1 Match the questions (1–5) with the answers (A–E).

1 Do we have to wear goggles in the pool? ....

2 Did Aaron have to play in the basketball match? ....

3 Does everyone have to wear a cycling helmet? ....

4 Did Hannah have to practise hard for the competition? ....

5 Does Mark have to pay for tennis lessons? ....

A Yes, he did. The team captain was sick.

B Yes, she did. She did three hours of gymnastics every day.

C Yes, they do. It can be dangerous when they're going very fast.

D No, he doesn't. His dad's the coach and so he teaches him for free.

E No, you don't have to, but the water can make your eyes red.

2 Complete the sentences with the correct form of *have to*.

1 The instructor says you .... wear goggles, but they can protect your eyes.

2 The park was closed, so the runners .... go somewhere else.

3 Nathan .... swim in a wetsuit because the sea is cold at the moment.

4 We .... go to bed now because the match starts very early tomorrow.

5 Ann .... buy a new tennis racket. She can have mine!

3 Put the words in the correct order to make questions.

1 join / could / Mr Smith / the judo club, / I?

....

2 you / me / a racket, / pass / please / can?

....

3 get / can / a towel / I / you?

....

4 you / tell / of the pool, / me / could / please / the opening times?

....

5 you / I / get / to try on / some helmets / could?

....

6 you / me / how / can / to hold / please / the racket correctly, / show?

....

4 🔊 7.8 Match the answers (A–F) with the questions in Ex 3 (1–6). Listen and check your answers.

A No, don't worry, I'm fine. I've got one in my bag. ....

B Yes, of course. 8.30 till 10.30 Monday to Friday and 9.30 till 7.30 at weekends. ....

C Yes, please. I'm looking for a cycling one. ....

D I'm sorry but there are no spaces left. You can come to the dance club instead. ....

E Sure, no problem. OK, you hold it here with your right hand and put your left hand there. ....

F Sure, here you are. ....

5 Complete the conversations with these phrases.

Can you help   Could I borrow   Could you
of course   Sorry, but   Sure, no problem
---

1 **A:** I don't have a wetsuit. .... one, please?

   B: Yes, ... We've got lots of different sizes.

2 **A:** .... me take down the badminton net, please?

   B: .... I have to catch my bus.

3 **A:** .... show me how to surf?

   B: .... Come to the beach with me on Saturday.

WRITING

1 Choose the correct words to complete the blog.

Last year I won the table **¹tennis / hockey** competition in our town. I played really well! I got a **²medal / money** for first place. At school I **³play / go** basketball and hockey. I'm better at basketball because I'm tall and I can run fast. I also go **⁴running / run** in the park near my house. Every day after school I **⁵do / play** badminton with my best friend. Next year we want to enter a local **⁶competition / practice** together. My friend is really good. I think we will win easily.

2 Read the blog in Ex 1 again. How many adverbs can you find?

3 Complete the sentences with adverbs formed from the adjectives in brackets.

1 He plays tennis .... (good).
2 Clare runs .... (fast).
3 David always arrives .... (late).
4 I play football .... (bad).
5 She won the race .... (easy).
6 She climbed up the mountain .... (slow).

4 Complete the conversations. Write one adverb for each gap.

1

Are you good at tennis?

No, I can't play it very ....

2
Are you always on time for class?

No, I often arrive ....

3
Can we speak loudly in the library?

No, we have to speak ....

4
Can you play the guitar?

Yes, but I play ....
because I never practise.

5 **e** Read the email. Choose the correct answer for each gap.

Hi Tara,

I had my first windsurfing lesson last week. It was really **¹**....... fun! At the beginning I did really **²**....... . I fell off the board into the sea so many times! It looked so **³**....... when I was watching the others windsurf. I did lots of practice. Then I **⁴**....... began to get better and I could stand on the board for longer. I couldn't believe how **⁵**....... you move when the wind blows! It was hard work and my arms and legs hurt the next day. My teacher said I did **⁶**....... for my first lesson. I'm going to have my next lesson tomorrow. I can't wait!

Speak soon,
Natalia

1 A good	**B** lots	**C** much
2 A bad	**B** badly	**C** worse
3 A easier	**B** easy	**C** easily
4 A slow	**B** slower	**C** slowly
5 A fast	**B** faster	**C** fastest
6 A good	**B** better	**C** well

6 Write an email to a friend. Tell your friend about a sport you learned to do. Remember to use adverbs and adjectives to describe your experience. Write 25 words or more.

UNIT CHECK

1 Complete the table.

noun	verb
cycling	1 ....
2	ski
surfing	3 ....
4	dive
skateboarding	5 ....
6	run

2 Complete the sentences with these words.

cycle   dived   ran   skied   surfed   swam

1 They took their boards to the beach and .... all morning.
2 Now that I have a new bike, I .... to school every morning.
3 Robbie .... from the boat to the island.
4 Chloe .... the fastest and won the marathon.
5 We .... really fast over the snow – it was great fun!
6 Did you see Tim? He just .... off the high board at the swimming pool.

3 Choose the correct words to complete the sentences.

1 I'm **doing / going** skiing with my aunt and uncle this winter.
2 I **went / played** hockey at school with my friends last Thursday.
3 Do you want to **go / do** gymnastics or play badminton?
4 Hannah **plays / does** judo at her local sports centre.
5 Jack's brother does hockey **practice / practise** every day after school.
6 We **played / went** cycling in the mountains when we were on holiday.

4 Complete the conversations with *practice* or the correct form of *practise*.

1
A: Hi, Helena. Are you ready for the badminton competition?
B: Not really! I had lots of homework and so I didn't have time to .... Did you?
A: Well, I .... a bit yesterday with my dad.

2
A: Are you coming to rugby ...., Joe?
B: No, I can't. I've got a music exam tomorrow and I have to ....

3
A: How did you become so good at golf, Jack?
B: Lots of ....!
A: Do you go to a golf club?
B: Yes, I do, but I often .... in my garden, too.

5 e Read the advert. Choose the correct answer for each gap.

bike racing club

Tuesdays, 4.30 p.m. @ the race track

.Can. you ride a bike? Do you enjoy cycling ¹....... ? Then why not join our club? You ²....... wear special clothing, just something warm and some trainers. You ³....... wear a helmet because it ⁴....... be dangerous. Racing club is £3 a week but you ⁵....... come the first week for free.

We hope to see you soon!

You ⁶....... be over fourteen years old to join the club.

	A Could	B Can	C Can't
1	A fast	B faster	C fastest
2	A don't have to	B didn't have to	C doesn't have to
3	A had to	B has to	C have to
4	A can	B can't	C couldn't
5	A can't	B couldn't	C can
6	A have to	B has to	C had to

REVIEW: UNITS 1–7

1 Read the clues and complete the crossword.

Across
2 things you put on your ears to listen to music
3 a person who plays music
6 the piece of paper a shop assistant gives you when you buy something

Down
1 a type of transport in the air, but not a plane
4 another word for a school student
5 something you sit on in a theatre or cinema

2 Complete the sentences with these words.

> bargain   documentary   ferry   printer   prize
> robots   screen   uniform

1 The first .... for the best photo competition is a new camera.

2 My eyes are tired. I need a break from my computer ....

3 Do you think one day we'll have .... that can do our homework?

4 My mum has to wear a .... for work. She works in a hospital.

5 I can't believe this wetsuit is half price. It's a real ....

6 Last night I watched a really interesting .... about tigers.

7 We wanted to take the .... to the island, but we didn't have any money left for our tickets.

8 I want to make two copies of my project. Can I use your .... ?

3 Complete the sentences with the correct form of the verbs in brackets.

1 You can't talk to Jack at the moment. He .... (have) a guitar lesson.

2 We .... (go out) to a pizza restaurant for Kirsty's birthday next week.

3 I can't wait. We .... (go) on holiday tomorrow.

4 Someone's ringing the doorbell. Wait here and I .... (see) who it is.

5 We .... (eat) our dinner when Rebecca called.

4 Choose the correct words to complete the conversation.

A: So, did you **¹enjoy / enjoying** the music festival at the weekend?

B: Yes, although the **²trip / journey** was really bad! It took us two hours to get there by car! There was a big cycling race and so we **³had to / have to** wait for the cyclists. Did you go?

A: Yes, we did. Luckily, we **⁴surfed the internet / checked online** the day before and read about the race. We took the train.

B: Good idea! Anyway the festival was awesome! I didn't see you there.

A: I saw you, but you **⁵danced / were dancing** with some friends.

B: Ah, maybe next time we can go together.

5 Read the email. Write the correct answer in each gap. Write one word for each gap.

Hi Laura,

You asked me about sports at my school. Well, my school is great for sports. Every week we have two **¹**.......................... lessons. In the summer we usually play tennis and volleyball. In the winter we often do gymnastics. **²**.......................... are also lots of after-school clubs. On Mondays there is **³**.......................... club. You can bring your bike to school. I don't do that club, but I go to swimming club **⁴**.......................... Tuesdays. I swim for the school team. We don't win many **⁵**.......................... , though! Every year we have a skiing trip to France. I went last year and skiied for the first time – I loved it! Our history teacher does judo and he **⁶**.......................... going to start a club next month. I really want to go to that club.

From,
Harriet

8 Wild world

READING

1 Match the words (1–6) with their meanings (A–F).

1 nature .... **3** igloo .... **5** climb ....
2 twice .... **4** freezing .... **6** probably ....

A move towards the top of something
B a house made of ice
C two times
D used as an answer when you think that something will happen or is true, although you're not sure
E very cold; this is when water becomes ice
F everything in the world that is not man-made, such as animals, plants and the weather

2 Read the article quickly. Who enjoys life on an island and who doesn't?

3 e Read the article again. For each question, choose the correct answer.

	Callum	Ben	Anna
Which person has done lots of activities with animals?	A	(B)	C
1 Which person moved to an island because of work?	A	B	C
2 Which person plans to leave their island for a few years?	A	B	C
3 Which person was born on their island?	A	B	C
4 Which person does a free time activity with family?	A	B	C
5 Which person buys things on the internet?	A	B	C
6 Which person lives in the coldest place?	A	B	C

4 Find words in the article that have these meanings.

1 think about something you want to do and decide how you will do it: ....
2 a very clever sea animal with a long grey pointed nose: ....
3 begin to be or feel something: ....
4 big in size, number or amount: ....
5 less than a particular number or amount: ....

Is it a thumbs up for island life?

A Callum

My family moved to the island of Unst when I was a baby. Unst is the furthest north you can live in the UK. Although we're north, it isn't freezing cold. It's often about five degrees in the winter. Just over 600 people live on Unst so life is different for teenagers here. I've never been to the cinema or been to a fast food restaurant. There are no clothes shops on Unst so I do all my shopping online. I'd like to go to university in Scotland or England. I plan to return here though. I can't think of a better place to live!

B Ben

I live on Roatan Island. My parents moved here for their jobs when I was three months old. There are cool things to do here. I've swum with dolphins and I've ridden horses on the beach. But I don't really enjoy island life now I'm a teenager. I've become a bit bored. When I finish school, I want to go and live with my auntie in New York. I can't wait to see my first snow! I'll probably come back for holidays.

C Anna

I'm from Iqaluit, on a large island in northern Canada. I've only been off the island once to visit Québec. Iqaluit means 'the place of many fish'. I love fishing and I often go out in my grandfather's boat. We've caught some really big fish together! For eight months of the year the temperature is below zero. I don't mind the cold. I love playing in the snow with my friends. A lot of my family live near our house, so I can walk and visit them whenever I want.

GRAMMAR

present perfect

1 Complete the table.

infinitive	past participle
begin	1 ....
read	2 ....
take	3 ....
hear	4 ....
wear	5 ....
buy	6 ....
write	7 ....

2 Put the words in the correct order to make sentences.

1 on holiday / hasn't / before / been / Finlay / in the UK

....
....

2 have / photos / taken / Max and Alana / of animals / lots of

....
....

3 spent / I've / in Italy / a summer

....
....

4 hasn't / on the back of / Oliver / ridden / a motorbike

....
....

5 on a fire / they've / their food / cooked

....
....

6 an interesting film / watched / about Russia / we've

....
....

3 Complete the sentences with the present perfect form of the verbs in brackets.

1 Annabelle .... (be) to Tunisia three times.
2 Jack and his sisters .... (visit) three continents.
3 My grandma .... (not swim) in the sea.
4 This is the first time Aliza .... (see) snow.
5 We .... (not have) a holiday in the mountains before.
6 I .... (not sleep) in a tent before.

4 🔊 8.1 Listen and complete the conversations.

1 **A:** So, you're going to Venezuela?
   B: Yes! I can't wait!
   A: Is it your first trip to South America?
   B: No, we .... there before.

2 **A:** How do you know so much about the South Pole, Kerry?
   B: We .... lots of books about Antarctica at school, Dad.

3 **A:** When is your sister going to Madrid?
   B: Next Tuesday. She's really excited. She .... always .... to go to Spain.

4 **A:** Does Richard know lots of people here?
   B: Yes, he .... this island many times. A lot of people on the island know him now.

5 **A:** Do you like mountain climbing?
   B: I love it! I .... the highest mountain in my country.

6 **A:** Where is Andrea going next month?
   B: Kenya and Tanzania. She .... through Asia and Europe and now she wants to go to Africa.

5 Complete the short answers. Then answer the questions for you.

1 **A:** Have you seen the Pyramids in Egypt?
   B: No, ...

2 **A:** Have you watched any good documentaries about the sea?
   B: Yes, ...

3 **A:** Has your best friend been to Brazil?
   B: No, ...

4 **A:** Has it snowed here before?
   B: No, ...

5 **A:** Have your parents visited more than two countries in Europe?
   B: Yes, ...

6 **A:** Has your granddad ever lived in another continent?
   B: Yes, ...

VOCABULARY

the natural world

1 Read the clues and complete the crossword.

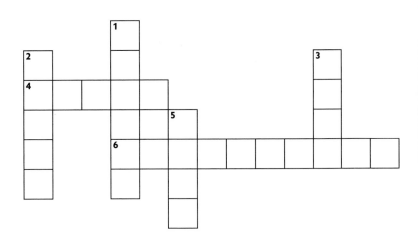

Across

4 the land next to the sea

6 a place with lots of very tall trees where it often rains

Down

1 a very dry place with lots of sand

2 a very large sea

3 a large area of water that has land all around it

5 a high area of land smaller than a mountain

4 🔊 8.2 Listen and repeat.

5 🔊 8.3 Listen, speak and record. Listen back and compare.

2 Complete the sentences with these adjectives.

cloudy   dry   icy   warm   wet   windy

1 It's freezing today and the footpath is very .... Be careful you don't fall over.

2 We can't have a picnic because it rained so much this morning. Everything is ....

3 It's really .... today. The sky's completely white and I can't see the sun at all.

4 It's very .... It's great weather for flying kites!

5 It was cold yesterday, but it's nice and .... today. You don't need your coat.

6 It's very .... in the desert because it never rains.

3 Look at A–G on the map and write the seven continents.

A North .... America ....

B S....................... A.......................

C E.......................

D Af.......................

E As.......................

F Au.......................

G An.......................

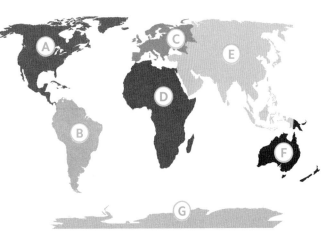

Extend

6 Complete the conversation with these words.

forest   insects   moon   rock   stars   wood

A: Did you go camping in the ¹.......................?

B: Well, there weren't many trees. It was more like a ²....................... .

A: Was it good fun?

B: Yes, it was. We did some ³....................... climbing in the day and at night we made a fire. There was a full ⁴....................... and the sky was really bright.

A: Cool! I love looking at ⁵....................... at night.

B: Why don't you come with us next time?

A: I don't like camping. I hate the idea of sleeping next to lots of ⁶....................... and other animals!

LISTENING

1 🔊 **8.4 Listen to a conversation and answer the questions.**

1 What is the relationship between the two people who are talking?

....

2 Lucy is doing a project for which school subject?

....

3 Where does Lucy want to go on holiday?

....

2 e 🔊 **8.5 Listen again. For each question, choose the correct answer.**

1 Lucy is doing a school project about

  A mountains.

  B rainforests.

  C rivers and lakes.

2 Lucy preferred the magazine photos because they

  A had the best colours.

  B were clearer.

  C looked more interesting.

3 Lucy's dad has

  A travelled on the Mississippi.

  B seen the Amazon.

  C been on the Nile.

4 How low can the night temperature be at Lake Victoria in June?

  A 15°C

  B 10°C

  C 2°C

5 Lucy's dad thinks that Lake Victoria

  A is an interesting place for a holiday.

  B is the most expensive place to go on holiday.

  C is a good place to get a job.

3 🔊 **8.6 Listen again and complete the sentences.**

1 Lucy's dad tells her that dinner will be ready in .... minutes.

2 Lucy's last geography project was about ....

3 Lucy's dad went on the Mississippi river when he was

....

4 Lake Victoria is the largest lake in ....

5 Lake Victoria is .... km long.

6 The rainy season ends in ....

present perfect with *ever* and *never*

4 **Make questions with the present perfect and *ever*.**

1 you / see / a full moon?

....

2 your teacher / be / to Australia?

....

3 your parents / go / mountain climbing?

....

4 your best friend / sleep / in a rainforest?

....

5 you / find / a mouse in your house?

....

6 you / swim / in the sea?

....

5 🔊 **8.7 Listen and repeat. Give short answers to the questions.**

Have you ever seen a full moon?

Yes, I have. / No, I haven't.

6 🔊 **8.8 Listen, speak and record. Listen back and compare.**

7 **Complete the sentences. Use *never* and the present perfect form of these verbs.**

climb   live   rain   ride   see   swim

1 Mark .... in an ocean.

2 Susan and Matthew .... a mountain.

3 It .... in this part of the desert.

4 My sister .... on an elephant, but it's something she really wants to do.

5 This snake .... in the wild. It was born in the zoo.

6 Lucien .... fog before. They don't have fog in his country.

SPEAKING

1 Match the questions (1–6) with the answers (A–F).

1 Have your mum and dad ever been to New York? ....

2 Has Charlie ever flown in a helicopter? ....

3 Have you ever held a snake? ....

4 Has Leo ever ridden a camel in the desert? ....

5 Have your grandparents ever lived on an island? ....

6 Have you ever seen a tiger in real life? ....

A No, I've never touched one. And I don't want to!

B Yes, they have. They both grew up in Jamaica.

C No, I've never seen any wild animals in real life.

D No, they haven't. They've never been to North America.

E No, he hasn't, but he has ridden an elephant.

F Yes, he has. His uncle flies one for his job.

2 Complete the sentences with *fun* or *funny*.

1 I always have .... when I go camping with friends.

2 The monkeys were so .... We all laughed when they stole the fruit from our table.

3 I think swimming in the sea is more .... than swimming in a pool.

4 The children have lots of .... outdoors when it snows.

5 Kiera watched a comedy about a bear. She thought it was very ....

6 It was really .... when my sister's hat fell into the river!

3 Choose the correct words to complete the sentences.

1 I think tigers are **scary / difficult** because of their big teeth.

2 Helena thinks wet weather is **boring / dangerous** because she has to stay indoors.

3 Freezing temperatures can be **healthy / dangerous** when you're not wearing the right clothes.

4 Swimming in the sea is good for you because the salt water is very **exciting / healthy**.

5 We had a **fantastic / strange** time in the desert. It was my best holiday ever!

6 It isn't a **strange / scary** animal. It's very friendly and likes being with people.

4 Choose the correct answer, A, B or C.

1 Jake has .... travelled in Europe.

   A never   **B** ever   **C** been

2 Have you ever .... in a snow storm?

   A went   **B** gone   **C** been

3 .... Rachel and Isaac ever walked in a rainforest?

   A Has   **B** Have   **C** Did

4 I .... never forgotten the first time I saw the ocean.

   A 've   **B** 'm   **C** has

5 My best friend has never .... a pet.

   A had   **B** has   **C** have

6 Have they ever .... a ferry across a lake?

   A take   **B** took   **C** taken

5 🔊 8.9 Listen to Zach and Ella talking about their plans for the day. Answer the questions.

1 What's the weather like?

....

2 Where do they decide to go?

....

6 🔊 8.10 Listen again and answer the questions.

What do Zach and Ella say about:

1 swimming in the river?

....

2 going to the coast?

....

3 walking to the lake for a swim?

....

4 going to the woods?

....

WRITING

1 Complete the postcard with these words.

boat   city   fog   highest   lake   Scotland

2 Write the words Emily uses in her postcard to describe these things.

her time in Scotland ..really good..

1 the places she has travelled to
....

2 Edinburgh Castle ....

3 mountain biking on Ben Nevis
.... , ...

4 the weather in Scotland ....

3 Look at these adjectives. Which are strong (S)? Which are not strong (N)?

1 noisy ....
2 terrifying ....
3 impossible ....
4 cold ....
5 hungry ....
6 freezing ....
7 busy ....
8 delicious ....
9 perfect ....
10 brilliant ....

Hi Matt,

I'm having a really good time in Scotland. We've travelled to lots of brilliant places. We started in Edinburgh, the capital of ¹............................. . I love Edinburgh. It has an amazing castle in the middle of the ²............................. . We've also been to the Highlands. We went mountain biking on Ben Nevis, Great Britain's ³............................. mountain. That was very exciting — and a bit scary! Yesterday we went to Scotland's most famous ⁴............................. , Loch Ness. We went on a ⁵............................. trip, but we didn't see the monster!

The weather is very strange here. We have had sun, rain and ⁶............................. — and it has snowed!

See you soon,
Emily

---

4 Complete the conversations with the adjectives in Ex 3.

1 How was your tip to Norway?

It was so cold, I was ....

2 Why didn't you like the beach?

I thought it was a bit ....
There were too many people!

3 Did you enjoy the boat trip?

No, it was awful. I'm scared of the ocean, so I thought it was ....

4 Did you eat anything for lunch?

No, so now I'm really ....!

5 **e** You are on a school trip. Write a postcard to a friend. Write about where you are, the activities and the weather. Use adjectives to make your postcard interesting and remember to begin and end in a friendly way. Write 25 words or more.

UNIT CHECK

1 **Choose the correct words to complete the sentences.**

1 Martin swam to the other side of the **lake / ocean** really fast.

2 We love playing in the **rainforest / park** near our house. It's great in the winter when it snows.

3 I'm really good at running. I can run up that **mountain / hill** in ten minutes.

4 We always go to this **island / desert** on holiday. It's always hot and sunny, and it's so green.

5 I've never been to the top of a **forest / mountain** because I don't like heights.

6 Juliette and her dad like going fishing in the **river / island**.

2 **Match 1–6 with A–F to make sentences.**

1 There were lots of insects under ....

2 My aunty lives by the sea ....

3 There wasn't a cloud in the sky, ...

4 There was ice on the car window ....

5 More than 2,000 different types of animal ....

6 The Atacama Desert is ....

A so we could see the moon clearly.

B the driest place in the world.

C because it was so cold.

D on the south coast of France.

E the rock.

F live in the Amazon rainforest.

3 **Complete the words in the sentences.**

1 There is so much f........................ today. I can't see where I'm going.

2 It's -5°C and very i........................ . Be careful when you walk outside – it's easy to fall.

3 Yesterday was really w........................ . Two trees fell down in my town.

4 I can't see any stars tonight. It's too c........................ .

5 The children don't want to play outside because it's f........................ c........................ .

6 We couldn't go on our boat trip because of the s........................ . The sea was too dangerous.

4 **Complete the interview with these words.**

> Asia   continents   snows   temperature   warmest   weather   world

A: Hi. I'm Martin from "Teen Travel" magazine and we're talking to teenagers from different cities around the ¹........................ . What's your name and where do you come from?

B: Hi. I'm Leyla and I come from Istanbul in Turkey.

A: So what's interesting about your city?

B: Well, Istanbul's unusual because it's in two ²........................ . The old part of the city is in Europe and the new part of the city is in ³........................ .

A: That is unusual! What's the ⁴........................ like in your city?

B: It changes at different times of the year. Well, in Istanbul summer starts in June and finishes in September. July is usually the ⁵........................ month. The ⁶........................ is usually around 28°C.

A: And does it get cold in Istanbul?

B: Not until the middle of December. It usually ⁷........................ in winter. The weather starts to get warmer again in March.

5 **Complete the interview. Write one word for each gap.**

How ADVENTUROUS are you, really?

Katie is a lucky fourteen-year-old. She ¹........................ been all over the world with her parents. We asked Katie to talk to us about some of her adventure holidays.

How many adventure holidays have you ²........................ on?

Six. I went on my first adventure holiday when I was seven.

Wow! Have you got a favourite holiday?

Not really. I ³........................ enjoyed all the holidays. I love animals, so our last holiday was fantastic – we went on safari in Tanzania.

Have you ⁴........................ had a scary experience on one of your adventure holidays?

Yes. When we were on safari in Tanzania an elephant ran towards our jeep. That was scary, but also amazing!

What kinds of activities have you ⁵........................ on holiday?

Well, my family loves extreme sports. We've been ice climbing in Canada, snowboarding in the desert in Dubai and surfing in Australia.

Fantastic! So why do you like adventure holidays so much?

You're never bored! I've seen lots of amazing places and done brilliant things on my holidays. I've ⁶........................ been on a beach holiday – and I don't want to! I love adventure holidays!

REVIEW: UNITS 1–8

1 Complete the conversations with these verbs.

buy   find   go   have   play   think

1 A: Do you often .... team sports?

   B: No, but I usually .... running after school.

2 A: Did Alistair .... an exam yesterday?

   B: Yes, he did. I .... he did well.

3 A: What did they .... at the shops?

   B: Nothing. They couldn't .... anything they liked.

2 Complete the questions with the correct form of the verbs in brackets.

1 .... you ever .... (play) cards on a beach?

2 .... Jake .... (take) any photos on holiday last week?

3 What .... you .... (do) at the moment?

4 When .... Simon usually .... (have) his lunch?

5 Where .... you first .... (meet) your best friend?

6 What .... Sam .... (write) about for his homework yesterday?

3 Complete the sentences with adverbs formed from the adjectives in brackets.

1 The giraffes moved .... (slow) in the hot weather.

2 The elephant hurt its foot and was walking .... (bad).

3 We couldn't hear the snake. It moved .... (quiet) through the rainforest.

4 The mouse escaped .... (easy) through the small hole in the wall.

5 Leopards are good at climbing. They can climb trees really .... (good).

6 Tigers can run very .... (fast) – often thirty-five miles an hour.

4 Choose the correct answer, A, B or C.

1 Jake .... when he started at our school, but now he's a really good swimmer.

   A had to swim   **B** couldn't swim   **C** has swum

2 David .... snow before. He comes from Botswana in Africa.

   A has never seen   **B** can see   **C** has to see

3 You .... lessons to learn how to surf, but it's a good idea.

   A can't take   **B** don't have to take   **C** couldn't take

4 Mountain biking .... dangerous so I always wear a helmet.

   A can be   **B** has to be   **C** couldn't be

5 I .... to Europe, but I would like to go one day.

   A have been   **B** went   **C** haven't been

6 We .... tennis at the moment because there isn't a net.

   A can't play   **B** have to play   **C** have played

5 Complete the conversation. Write one word for each gap.

A: Have you heard of Blackwood Activity Centre?

B: **1** ...., I haven't. What can you do there?

A: Lots of things. You **2** .... do horse-riding, kiteboarding, rock climbing and judo.

B: So, **3** .... you been there?

A: Yes, I went last Saturday.

B: What did you do?

A: I wanted to go windsurfing, **4** .... we couldn't because it was too windy.

B: I thought it has **5** .... be windy for kiteboarding.

A: It does, but when it's very windy, it can **6** .... dangerous. I did judo instead – I really enjoyed it.

READING

1 Complete the sentences with these words.

| chef | clip | doll | instructions | series | tiny |

1 My brother is learning to be a .... One day he'd like his own restaurant.

2 This small .... is my little sister's favourite toy.

3 This video .... is really funny. A monkey comes into the house and steals the cake.

4 She had a .... bedroom. It was only big enough for her bed and a very small table.

5 We watched a .... of programmes about Indian food.

6 I don't know how to cook this food. Are there any .... on the box?

2 Look at the photo and read the article quickly. What is it about?

A a way to use less plastic   **B** a different kind of food

Eat with it ... then eat it!

by Sam Mayers

We use too much plastic. It's a fact. If you eat in a café or fast food restaurant, you'll usually use some plastic. Maybe you'll get a plastic spoon with your ice cream or a plastic cup for your orange juice. We eat and drink and then throw the plastic in the bin. The problem with all this plastic is that it stays on the planet for hundreds of years. Although everyone knows this, we continue buying fast food because we love it and it saves us time.

So if you care about the world, but you like to eat fast food, you'll love this idea. How about a spoon that you can eat after you use it? A company in India has found a good way to use less plastic. The company has made edible spoons. This means spoons that you can eat.

These edible spoons are very strong. You can even use them with hot soup or coffee. If you eat your soup with one, the spoon won't go soft. So, are the spoons sweet or salty? They can be both. The company makes them in different flavours. I think this is a great idea. You can choose a sweet spoon for your desserts and a salty spoon for your main course.

If the Indian company can make the spoons cheaply, we'll soon see them in our local cafés. If the spoons work well, maybe we'll find ways to make plates and bowls you can eat too!

3 **e** Read the article again. For each question, choose the correct answer.

1 Why does Sam say plastic cups and spoons are bad?

  A People drop them on the floor.

  B They stay on the planet for a long time.

  C People put them in rubbish bins.

2 Sam says people use plastic a lot because

  A they don't know it's bad for the planet.

  B they are busy and it makes life easier.

  C they don't like eating at home.

3 How do we know the edible spoons are strong?

  A It's difficult to break them.

  B You can put heavy things on them.

  C They don't change shape when hot.

4 What does Sam like about the edible spoons?

  A They are not all the same.

  B You can use them to eat desserts.

  C They have salt in them.

5 Why are the edible spoons not in lots of shops now?

  A They are not as cheap as plastic spoons.

  B People don't want spoons they can eat.

  C The Indian company can't make enough.

4 Match sentences 1–6 with sentences A–F.

1 The sun is actually a star. ....

2 I don't need this anymore. ....

3 I don't like swimming in the sea. ....

4 My sister's a manager. ....

5 There's a lot of sugar in this tea. ....

6 We don't travel far to school. ....

A It's too sweet for me.

B The salty sea water hurts my eyes.

C It's not a planet.

D We go to the local school.

E She works for a company that makes chocolate.

F Can you put it in the bin, please?

GRAMMAR

first conditional

1 Match 1–6 with A–F to make sentences.

1 If I have time, ...
2 Emma won't be late ....
3 If Grace doesn't finish her dinner, ...
4 My teacher will be unhappy ....
5 If you like Japanese food, ...
6 The party will be inside ....

A if she leaves now.
B you'll love this sushi restaurant.
C if I don't do my homework.
D I'll bake her a birthday cake.
E if the weather is bad.
F she'll be hungry later.

2 🔊 **9.1 Listen to Alex talking to his dad. What does Alex want to do?**

3 🔊 **9.2 Complete the sentences from the recording with the correct form of the verbs in brackets. Listen again and check your answers.**

1 Dad, ... you .... (let) me have a party if I .... (do) well in my school exams?
2 If I .... (have) a party, we .... (stay) in the garden.
3 If everyone .... (bring) some food, it .... (not cost) much at all.

4 Complete the first conditional sentences with the correct form of the verbs in brackets.

1 If we .... (have) pizza for lunch, I .... (be) really happy.
2 You .... (be) thirsty if you .... (not take) a bottle of water with you.
3 My mum .... (phone) me if I .... (need) to get home for dinner.
4 They .... (put) the tables outside the café if it .... (be) sunny.
5 If you .... (eat) all the cake now, there .... (not be) any for later.
6 If Aidan .... (like) cooking, he .... (love) this new cooking blog.

5 Put the words in the correct order to make sentences.

1 see / I / time tomorrow, /I'll / If / my friends / have

....

2 I'll / snows tomorrow / really happy if / it / be

....

3 some fruit / I'm / eat / hungry later, / If / I'll

....

4 if / will / there's / text me / a party / My friends

....

5 for a swim / the weather's good tomorrow, / go / If / I'll

....

6 I / feel ill / too many sweets, / If / I'll / eat

....

6 Complete the sentences to make them true for you.

1 If I have time tomorrow, I'll ....
2 I'll be really happy if ....
3 If I'm hungry later, I'll ....
4 My friends will text me if ....
5 If the weather's good tomorrow, I'll ....
6 If I eat too many sweets, I'll ....

73

VOCABULARY

food and health

1 Complete the words in the sentences.

1 I usually have a bowl of c........................ for breakfast in the morning.

2 When he gets home from school, Joe always has a drink and a b........................ .

3 My favourite meal is b........................ and chips.

4 I never eat o........................ because I don't like eggs.

5 My uncle's Italian and he cooks the best p........................ dishes!

2 Look at the pictures. Complete the sentences with the correct form of these verbs.

bake   barbecue   boil   fry   grill   roast

1 Noah .... some bread at school yesterday.

2 Can you .... some water for the vegetables, please?

3 My dad enjoys .... in the summer.

4 Mum's in the kitchen. She .... a chicken for dinner.

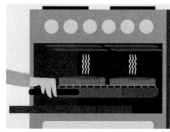

5 We always .... our meat. It's healthier that way.

6 I .... the chicken for the salad this morning.

3 🔊 9.3 Listen and complete the sentences.

1 If I don't have ...., I'm really hungry by ten o'clock.

2 I usually eat .... for breakfast.

3 Why don't you get .... ?

4 If you do ...., you'll feel better.

5 Do you want to go ...., Sophie?

6 You need to find ...., too.

4 Choose the correct words to complete the conversations.

1 A: Are you OK? Your eyes and nose are red!
   B: No, I'm not. I've got a **stomach ache / cold**. I feel terrible!

2 A: Do you want some of this chocolate cake?
   B: I can't. I've got really bad **toothache / headache** and it hurts when I eat.

3 A: I can't believe you ate two burgers!
   B: Never again! I've got **stomach ache / a cold** now.

4 A: Have I got a **temperature / toothache**?
   B: Yes, it's 39°C. You're very hot. I'll give you some medicine.

5 A: Why don't you want to go on the ferry?
   B: Boat journeys make me feel **stomach ache / sick**!

6 A: Why have you got your eyes closed?
   B: I've got a bad **headache / stomach ache** and the light makes it feel worse.

5 🔊 9.4 Listen to conversations 1–3 from Ex 4. Practise the conversations.

6 🔊 9.5 Listen, speak and record. Listen back and compare.

Extend

7 Match these words with their meanings (1–5).

butter   chilli   garlic   honey   toast

1 a yellow food that you put on bread or use in cooking: ....

2 something sweet that bees make: ....

3 grilled bread: ....

4 a small thin red or green vegetable with a very hot taste: ....

5 a small white vegetable like an onion with a very strong smell: ....

LISTENING

1 🔊 **9.6** Listen to a telephone message. Why doesn't Carla know all the information about the school picnic?

2 🔊 🔊 **9.7** Listen again. For each question, write the correct answer in each gap. Write one word or a number or a date or a time.

School picnic

Day: __Saturday__

Place: on ¹ .... Road

Time to arrive: ² ....

Food to take: ³ ....

Wear: ⁴ ....

Miss Sharp's tel. no.: ⁵ ....

3 🔊 **9.8** Listen again and answer the questions.

1 Why did the day of the picnic change?

....

2 What time are they planning to eat the picnic?

....

3 How is Lisa planning to travel to the picnic?

....

4 What time is Lisa leaving her house on Saturday?

....

5 What did the teacher give everyone?

....

6 What food is Lisa bringing to the picnic?

....

7 Who's going to bake a cake?

....

8 Who's organising the picnic?

....

advice: *should*

4 Complete the sentences with *should* or *shouldn't* and the verbs in brackets.

You look hot. You _should have_ (have) a cold drink.

1 Mark is very tired. He .... (get) more sleep.

2 You .... (ask) Sam to help you with your homework. He's good at maths.

3 Jack .... (go) swimming today. He's got a bad cold.

4 Alice .... (enter) the cooking competition. She isn't very good.

5 My dad .... (put) so much salt on his food. It's very unhealthy.

6 William and Ben .... (leave) home earlier. They're always late for school.

5 Complete the tips with *should* or *shouldn't* and these verbs.

---

forget   invite   make sure   play   tell   think

Recipe for a great party!

- You ¹ .... a good group of friends. You can't have a good party without a good group of people.

- Be careful how you invite your friends. You ² .... people about your party on a social networking site. You don't want hundreds of people to arrive at your party!

- You ³ .... that everyone has enough to eat and drink. If you don't have much money to spend on the party, you ⁴ .... about asking friends to bring some food and drink, too.

- Good music is very important. You don't have to get a DJ, but you ⁵ .... a good variety of music.

- Lastly, you ⁶ .... to take some photos – they're a great way to remember the party!

SPEAKING

1 🔊 9.9 **Listen and complete the conversations.**

1 A: I can't sleep because I've got an important football match tomorrow.

   B: You ¹........................... .

2 A: I feel so sick!

   B: I'm not surprised! You ²........................... .

3 A: My toothache is getting worse.

   B: I really think you ³........................... .

4 A: Where's Harry? The film will start soon.

   B: I don't know. Maybe we ⁴........................... .

5 A: I'd really like to learn to play the guitar.

   B: You ⁵........................... . He's a guitar teacher.

6 A: Have you seen the time? It's nearly eight o'clock.

   B: Really? I ⁶........................... . I don't want to be late for school again.

2 🔊 9.10 **Look at the photos and listen to Lucas and Rosa. Which is Rosa's favourite activity? Which activity does Lucas like best?**

3 🔊 9.11 **Listen again and complete the sentences.**

1 I enjoy reading because it ....

2 I don't really like the gym because I don't like ....

3 I love being outdoors because .... makes me feel good.

4 Not really, because I .... cooking.

5 I like playing my guitar best because music ....

6 My .... baking because I love making food for my friends and family.

4 **Put the words in the correct order to make sentences.**

1 should / fresh air and exercise / have / lots of / children

....

2 too much / people / sugar / eat / shouldn't

....

3 should / part of / your main meal / vegetables / be

....

4 fried food / you / eat / a lot of / shouldn't

....

5 eat / every day / everyone / fresh fruit / should

....

6 drive less / walk more / people / and / should

....

WRITING

1 Match the comments (1–6) with the advice (A–F).

1 Sam feels tired.

2 We're bored.

3 Dan has stomach ache.

4 My brother is hungry.

5 Francis has toothache.

6 I feel sick.

A You should go for a walk.

B He should have a good breakfast.

C He should find time to relax.

D You should lie down for a while.

E She should see a dentist.

F He should eat less fried food.

2 Complete the sentences with *because* or *so*.

1 Sam's going to bed .... he's got a temperature.

2 I'm hungry, ... I'm going to have a snack.

3 We went out for pizza .... it was Sara's birthday.

4 I'm bored, ... I'm going to my friend's house.

5 My brother doesn't like sweet things, ... I ate his cake.

6 They felt sick .... they ate too much ice cream.

3 Look at the pictures (A–C). Match these words with the pictures.

---

black   chat   ~~decide~~   forget   grandma
mobile phone   surprise   terrible   upset

A ....decide...... , ... , ...

B .... , ... , ...

C .... , ... , ...

4 **e** Look at the pictures again. Write the story shown in the pictures. Write 35 words or more.

UNIT CHECK

1 **Choose the correct words to complete the sentences.**

1 Tom won't arrive on time if he **'ll leave / doesn't leave** now.

2 If I **have / 'll have** enough money, I'll buy you an ice cream.

3 If he goes to bed early, he **feels / 'll feel** better.

4 If they **finish / will finish** their homework early, they'll watch a film.

5 You **catch / 'll catch** a cold if you don't wear your coat.

6 Alice **stays / will stay** at home if her headache gets worse.

2 **Complete the phrases about not feeling well with *a, e, i* or *u*.**

have a c o ld

1 have a h.... ....d....ch....

2 have s t....m....ch ....ch....

3 have a t....mp....r....t....r

4 have t.... ....th....ch....

5 feel s....ck

3 **Choose the correct words to complete the sentences.**

1 My brother **does / makes** exercise every day.

2 I love **desserts / snacks**. My favourite is a packet of crisps.

3 Can you pass me a **spoon / knife** for my soup, please?

4 A **healthy / fresh** meal should have vegetables in it.

5 My dad loves barbecued **steak / omelette**.

6 Dan has **stomach ache / a temperature** because he ate too quickly.

4 **Complete the conversation with these words.**

bake   cooking   doing   if   should   so   will

A: What are you ¹........................ at the weekend?

B: Well, ²........................ it's sunny, we'll have a picnic on the beach. How about you?

A: It's my grandpa's eightieth birthday, ³........................ we're having a big party on Sunday. We'll ⁴........................ the cake and get the food ready on Saturday.

B: Are you ⁵........................ anything?

A: If I cook the food, no one ⁶........................ want to eat it! I'll help make the salads on Sunday.

B: You ⁷........................ learn to cook. It's not that hard and it's fun.

A: Maybe one day.

5 **e** **Read the email. Write the correct answer in each gap. Write one word for each gap.**

Hi Anna

Sorry I <u>couldn't</u> come to your party. I felt really ill. It started ¹........................ Thursday night. I felt sick and ²........................ stomach ache. I thought it was ³........................ I ate a big chocolate cake for dessert, but it wasn't that. That night I had ⁴........................ temperature. I was so hot! I also had a bad headache. In the morning my mum took me ⁵........................ the doctor's. The doctor said I just had a cold. I stayed ⁶........................ bed for the whole weekend. I was so bored! I hope we can meet up soon. I want to give you your birthday present.

Love,
Lucy

REVIEW: UNITS 1–9

1 Match these words with their meanings (1–6).

bargain   drawing   museum   ruler   screen   wood

1 a building where people can go and see important objects from history: ....

2 the part of a computer where the picture or information appears: ....

3 a flat piece of plastic, wood, or metal that you use for drawing straight lines: ....

4 a group of trees that is smaller than a forest: ....

5 a picture you make with a pen or pencil: ....

6 something you buy cheaply or for less than its usual price: ....

2 Choose the correct answer.

1 Have you ever been to France?
 A Yes, I have been.
 B Yes, twice.
 C Yes, I'm going next month.

2 Have you got any smaller trainers?
 A Yes, they're smaller.
 B Sorry, we don't have larger ones.
 C Just a minute. I'll have a look.

3 Will you help me with my homework, please?
 A Yes, if I have time.
 B Sorry, I don't have any homework.
 C I can't do your homework.

4 Do you often go swimming?
 A Yes, I do.
 B Yes, I have.
 C Yes, I swim.

5 How did you get home yesterday?
 A We got home early.
 B On foot
 C We waited on the platform.

6 Why are you carrying that racket?
 A We've got a diving competition at school.
 B I've got hockey practice.
 C I'm playing badminton with my friend.

3 e Read the text. Choose the correct answer for each gap.

Recipe for teen talent

I love 'The Great Cooking Contest'. It's like a talent _show_ for teenage cooks. Ten teenagers take part and every week they **1**...... cook different things. They do the cooking in a TV studio **2**...... lots of people. At the end of the show they **3**...... marks for their cooking. There are four people who give marks. Three of them are famous **4**......, but one person is a famous comedian. She's really **5**...... . I think this is the best cooking **6**...... on TV!

	A TV	**B** show	**C** game
1	**A** have to	**B** should	**C** like
2	**A** between	**B** behind	**C** in front of
3	**A** get	**B** make	**C** do
4	**A** cookers	**B** chefs	**C** beginners
5	**A** fun	**B** funnier	**C** funny
6	**A** competition	**B** practice	**C** prize

4 Complete the conversation with the correct form of these verbs.

be   go   have   see   show   stay   visit

A: Hi, Rosie. How are you?

B: Hi, Ben. Great, thanks. I've just come back from holiday.

A: Really? Where **1**........................ you .... ?

B: France. We went on holiday there for two weeks. We **2**........................ a great time. **3**........................ you ever .... to France?

A: No, I haven't. We always **4**........................ my uncle in Greece. Did you go camping in France?

B: No, we **5**........................ in a really nice apartment. My bedroom had views of the sea. It was fantastic!

A: Did you just go with your parents?

B: Yes, but we met a really nice family. I spent a lot of time with the daughter, Ella. Hopefully we **6**........................ them again next year. Did you have a good holiday at your uncle's?

A: Yes, thanks. We went to a kite festival – some of the kites were amazing. I **7**........................ you my photos next time I see you.

READING AND WRITING

Part 1

For each question, choose the correct answer.

1

SWIMMING POOL

£4.50 / children under twelve £2.50
Half price tickets on Mondays

A Swimming costs less on Mondays.
B Eleven-year-olds pay the same as adults.
C Young children swim for free.

2

 ✕

Hi Zoe,
I've got two tickets for the cinema tonight.
I booked online, so I got the tickets cheaper.
Do you want to go?
Ella

A Ella wants to tell Zoe about a website that sells cheap tickets.
B Ella is inviting Zoe to the cinema.
C Ella thinks that booking online is a good idea.

3

```
Man's watch for sale –
needs new battery

£30 – cash only
Phone 0789 375 542
```

A You can pay by cheque.
B You need to change a part of the watch.
C The watch that's for sale is for a child.

4

Oliver,
Our surfing lesson is at 10 a.m. on Saturday.
I'll come to your house at 9.30 a.m. and we
can walk to the beach together.
Pete

A Pete wants Oliver to go for a walk on the beach.
B Pete wants Oliver to learn to surf.
C Pete wants to arrive at the surfing lesson with Oliver.

5

Special offer!
Buy a burger and get a drink
free! Every Wednesday!

A You can only buy burgers on Wednesdays.
B You pay less for a burger and drink on Wednesdays.
C You have to buy a drink with your burger.

6

Hi Max,
What's our geography homework? I lost
the piece of paper with it on. I think it was
something about rivers.
Thanks,
Ali

Why did Ali write this message?
A to ask Max what the homework is
B to tell Max he lost his homework
C to let Max know the homework is about rivers

Part 2

For each question, choose the correct answer.

	Talia	Sebastian	Rowan
7 Which person often does their sport with someone in their family?	A	B	C
8 Which person first started playing their sport at school?	A	B	C
9 Which person had an accident when they were playing their sport?	A	B	C
10 Which person wants to study sport in the future?	A	B	C
11 Which person met a famous sports person?	A	B	C
12 Which person is planning to buy some new equipment?	A	B	C
13 Which person has taught other people their sport?	A	B	C

WE ♥ SPORT!

A Talia

I love volleyball. I play for my school team, but I first played volleyball on holiday. I was in Italy with my cousins and some local Italian children taught us how to play. My cousins still play volleyball and we often practise together. At the moment we're training for a big competition. We lost the last one, so I hope we'll win this time! When I'm older, I want to go to university and train to be a P.E. teacher.

B Sebastian

I love playing tennis. My first experience of it was at primary school. Now I belong to a club. A famous tennis player was a member of the club, but that was years before I joined. I usually go to the club twice a week, but I can't play at the moment. I hurt my foot last week when I was playing tennis. I often help our coach and I give lessons to beginners.

C Rowan

I really love skiing. I first skied on holiday with my family. Some people say it's a dangerous sport, but I haven't had any accidents. Luckily, I live near mountains so I can ski at the weekends. I'm going on a school skiing trip next month and I need to buy some new goggles. Once when I was skiing, I met the world number-one Olympic skier. My friends couldn't believe it!

Part 3

For each question, choose the correct answer.

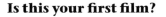

'The Dark Forest' is a fantastic new horror film coming to cinemas later this week.

Our journalist, Dan Ashton, went to meet the young star of the film, Naomi Smith.

Is this your first film?

The first of many, I hope! People think I've done a lot of acting on TV. The truth is someone saw me on stage at my local theatre and asked me to go to the film studio. They liked my acting and asked me to be in the film.

What happened to your school work while you were making the film?

I couldn't go to school or do lots of homework as I was too busy. I really missed my school friends. The film company organised a special teacher for me and I had lessons every day. I think my parents were worried about school at first, but now they're happy that I did the film. They can't believe the good luck I've had this year!

What did you enjoy the most about making this film?

I loved it all! I really enjoyed learning how to act better. I learned so much! But probably the thing I'll remember forever is meeting my favourite actors, Joss Parker and Rosalind Knight. I also travelled to some amazing places to film different parts of the film.

Thank you, Naomi, and I look forward to seeing you in the film.

14 *The Dark Forest* is
  A a scary film on at cinemas now.
  B a film that has been on at the cinema for a week.
  C a film that will be at cinemas in a few days.

15 What acting has Naomi done in the past?
  A She's been on TV.
  B She's been in a play.
  C She's been in a film.

16 What does Naomi say about her school work when they were making the film?
  A She missed a lot of studying.
  B She did lots of extra homework.
  C She had a new teacher.

17 Naomi says that her parents
  A worry about her school work.
  B think she's very lucky.
  C are excited about her future.

18 What does Naomi say she'll never forget?
  A the people she met
  B the places she visited
  C the things she learned

Part 4

For each question, choose the correct answer for each gap.

Jamie Oliver

Jamie Oliver is a famous TV chef. He was born in Essex in the UK. Jamie's **(19)** .... job was in an Italian restaurant in London. He then worked at The River Café. He was working there when a TV company saw him. They liked Jamie and **(20)** .... him to do a cooking show on TV. His TV show was very **(21)** .... and he soon began writing cook books. You can find his cook books in many different languages. As well as writing books, Jamie has opened restaurants in the UK and in other **(22)** .... He has also helped **(23)** .... the food in British schools. He wants children to eat healthier food and be interested in cooking. Jamie is one of the richest and most successful chefs in the **(24)** ....

19 **A** beginning   **B** early   **C** first
20 **A** asked   **B** said   **C** talked
21 **A** favourite   **B** popular   **C** loved
22 **A** cities   **B** towns   **C** countries
23 **A** improve   **B** repair   **C** discuss
24 **A** history   **B** world   **C** life

Part 5

For each question, write the correct answer in each gap. Write one word for each gap.

Example: having

From: Leila
To: Ben

Hi Ben,

How are you? I'm .... a great time in Paris. We've been **(25)** .... a boat trip along the River Seine and we've climbed to the top of the Eiffel Tower. Today we **(26)** .... going to visit a museum. The weather's **(27)** .... really good. At the moment it's warm and sunny. I love the cafés in Paris. Every day we go to **(28)** .... different café. Yesterday I bought a new jacket. The shops here are much better **(29)** .... at home. I'm trying **(30)** .... practise my French, too! It's fun, but I'm not sure people always understand me!

Speak soon,
Leila

Part 6

You want to go to the cinema on Friday with your English friend, Joe.

Write an email to Joe.

In the email:

- **ask** Joe **to go to the cinema with you** on Friday
- say **what** you want **to watch** at the cinema
- say **how** you will **travel there**.

Write **25 words** or more.

....

Part 7

Look at the three pictures.

Write the story shown in the pictures.

Write **35 words** or more.

....

LISTENING

Part 1

🔊 10.1 **For each question, choose the correct picture.**

....

1 What's Lucy going to buy her teacher?

 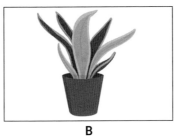 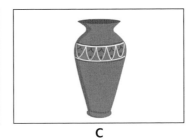

| A | B | C |

2 What time does judo club start?

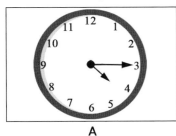 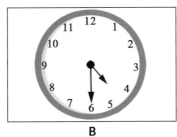 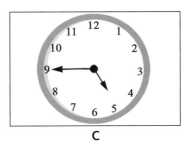

| A | B | C |

3 Which girl is Tom's sister?

  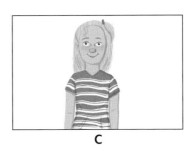

| A | B | C |

4 What was the weather like on the beach yesterday?

| A | B | C |

5 How much is the school trip?

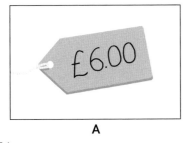  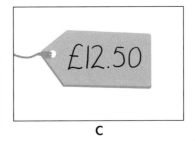

| A | B | C |

Part 2

🔊 10.2 For each question, write the correct answer in the gap. Write one word or a number or a date or a time.

You will hear a teacher telling students about a theatre trip.

School theatre trip

Name of theatre: ..... Adelphi .....

Date of trip: **(6)** ....

Meet outside: **(7)** ....

Leave at: **(8)** .... a.m.

Travel by: **(9)** ....

Do not take: **(10)** ....

Part 3

🔊 10.3 For each question, choose the correct answer.

You will hear Isobel talking to her friend Finlay about an art lesson she had.

....

11 Who taught the art lesson?

   A a teacher from school

   B a local artist

   C a parent of a student

12 What did they do in the lesson yesterday?

   A They painted.

   B They drew.

   C They took photos.

13 What do students have to bring to the lessons?

   A art equipment

   B an old shirt

   C a big folder

14 Isobel thought the first art lesson was

   A too short.

   B a bit difficult.

   C quite boring.

15 How does Finlay feel about next week's art lesson?

   A upset

   B excited

   C worried

Part 4

🔊 10.4 **For each question, choose the correct answer.**

16 You will hear a phone message from Rosie's mum.
   What does she want Rosie to do?
   A collect her sister
   B come home early
   C go to the shops

17 You will hear two friends talking about their day.
   What did they enjoy the most?
   A swimming
   B playing a team sport
   C eating something sweet

18 You will hear a teacher talking to his class about a story.
   What does he want the class to do?
   A plan their story well
   B think of a true story
   C write a long story

19 You will hear a girl, Martha, talking to her friend.
   Why did Martha miss the party?
   A She had toothache.
   B She had a temperature.
   C She had stomach ache.

20 You will hear a boy, Liam, talking about his holiday.
   What activity did he try for the first time?
   A sailing
   B windsurfing
   C fishing

Part 5

🔊 10.5 **For each question, choose the correct answer.**

You will hear Alice talking to her grandad about an activity holiday. Which activity did she do on each day?

Example:
Sunday   H

Days
21 Monday   ....
22 Tuesday   ....
23 Wednesday   ....
24 Thursday   ....
25 Friday   ....

Activities
A badminton
B basketball
C climbing
D cycling
E horse riding
F sailing
G swimming
H table tennis

SPEAKING

Part 1

Phase 1

🔊 10.6 The examiner is going to ask you some questions about you. Listen and answer the questions. Pause the recording after each beep and give your answer.

Phase 2

🔊 10.7 Now the examiner is going to ask you some questions about holidays. Listen and answer the questions. Pause the recording after each beep and give your answer.

Part 2

Phase 1

🔊 10.8 The examiner is going to give you some photos. You and the other student must talk about them together. Listen and follow the examiner's instructions. Talk together for about 1–2 minutes.

🔊 10.9 Now the examiner is going to ask you some questions about the topic in the photos. Listen and answer the questions. Pause the recording after each beep and give your answer.

Phase 2

🔊 10.10 The examiner is going to ask you some more questions about the topic in the photos. Listen and answer the questions. Pause the recording after each beep and give your answer.

Do you like these free time activities?

AUDIOSCRIPTS

S.1

1 I go to the same school as my cousin and we play football together. I don't see his brother James a lot because he's at university now.

2 I love going fishing with my grandpa. He doesn't live near us. We visit him and grandma Alice in the school holidays. Everyone says I look like him!

3 Most of the time we're good friends! We share the same bedroom. We're twins. We're fourteen and our sister's sixteen.

4 I love her cakes! She's a great cook – maybe that's why my uncle eats so much! When I visit my cousins, she always makes us chocolate cake. It's yummy!

S.4 and S.5

1
A: How do you spell 'aunty'?
B: A–U–N–T–Y.

2
A: How do you spell 'address'?
B: A–D–D–R–E–S–S.

3
A: How do you spell 'surname'?
B: S–U–R–N–A–M–E.

4
A: How do you spell 'clock'?
B: C–L–O–C–K.

5
A: How do you spell 'birthday'?
B: B–I–R–T–H–D–A–Y.

6
A: How do you spell 'cousin'?
B: C–O–U–S–I–N.

7
A: How do you spell 'money'?
B: M–O–N–E–Y.

8
A: How do you spell 'shelf'?
B: S–H–E–L–F.

9
A: How do you spell 'cupboard'?
B: C–U–P–B–O–A–R–D.

10
A: How do you spell 'cushion'?
B: C–U–S–H–I–O–N.

1.3–1.5

Hi, Jacob. It's Matt here. I'm calling about the street dancing classes. Are you still interested? They start this week and they're every Tuesday after school. They begin at 4.15 p.m. and finish at 5.45 p.m. You can pay for a group of lessons or pay every week. Six lessons are thirty pounds or you can pay five pounds fifty per lesson. The school's in the centre of town. It's on Station Street, next to the shopping centre. It's easy to find. It has a large red door and the name of the school is City Dance. The teacher's name is Mark Rowlands. That's R–O–W–L–A–N–D–S. He's a brilliant dancer. He dances in music videos! You can watch him on YouTube. You phone the school to book a place in the class. The number is 0145 277 656. It's a good idea to phone soon because his classes are always popular. You can wear any clothes, but remember to bring water. I hope you can come! Bye!

2.2

I = Interviewer   R = Ross

I: How much technology does your family use, Ross?

R: My brother and I have a tablet each. We often send emails and stream films.

I: How about your parents?

R: My dad doesn't like computers, but he does have a laptop. He needs it for work. My mum uses her mobile phone all the time. She often downloads music and chats to my aunty online.

I: Thanks, Ross. Do you want us to visit your school next week? Then let us know. You can leave a message on the radio station website. Our address is www.lunaradio. com. That's L–U–N–A–R–A–D–I–O dot com.

2.3 and 2.4

1
A: Hi, Holly. What are you hoping to get for your birthday?

B: Well, my sister's got this really cool tablet. I'm hoping to get one of those, but they are quite expensive.

A: But you've got a laptop – and it's really new!

B: I know, but it's so heavy! And my mobile phone is too small for watching films and things.

A: True!

2
A: Look, there's my computer teacher, Mr McGuire. He's walking into the supermarket.

B: The man in the T-shirt, Harriet?

A: No! He's not that young! Can you see the man in the jacket and T-shirt? That's him. He's standing next to the man with the funny tie.

B: Oh, I know that teacher! He's really nice.

3
A: Hi, Maisy. What are you doing?

B: I'm looking at some websites for my homework.

A: Cool. I'm doing my homework on famous painters. What are you doing?

B: I'm writing about famous singers in my country. Look at these photos! They're amazing! Have you got a printer? I want to use these photos in my homework.

A: Yes, you can use it after school.

4
A: Hi. Can I speak to Charlie, please?

B: Oh hi, Evie. Sorry, Charlie's talking to his brother online. His brother's in Russia at the moment.

A: Ah yes, I remember. Can I call him in half an hour, at a quarter past six?

B: Mmm … actually, can you call back at six o'clock? Charlie's got a piano lesson at six thirty.

5
A: So, Adam, my brother's got these speakers – they're really good.

B: I need some speakers for my laptop. How much are they? It says £7.49 here.

A: That's the price for the webcams. The speakers are £14.99. How much money have you got?

B: Only £10.50 Never mind.

A: We can look in another shop.

3.2–3.4

B = Ben   A = Ava

B: Hi, Ava. What are you doing?

A: My geography homework. We're studying education around the world. Last week we read about schools in Russia and Argentina. Yesterday we watched a film about Bangladesh in our geography lesson. It was about boat schools.

B: Sounds cool.

A: Yes, our geography films are usually boring, but this one wasn't. The lesson went really quickly.

B: So why were there schools on boats?

A: Because in the rainy season the normal schools on land closed because of all the water and flooding. In dry weather they didn't need these schools.

B: Right. But how did the students get to school?

A: The boat was also like a school bus. It picked students up from their houses. Then it stopped somewhere and classes began.

B: But you can't have computers and stuff on a boat. There's no electricity. How did they work? Did they use big batteries?

A: You're right, there wasn't any electricity like in a normal school. They were solar-powered – they used the energy from the sun. No need for batteries!

B: And how many students studied on these boats?

A: Each boat had a classroom for about thirty-five students. I'd love to go to school on a boat!

B: I'd like to visit one for a day, but not every day. I prefer schools on land!

3.5

R = Rebecca   M = Max

R: Do you remember your first day at this school, Max?

M: Yes, I do.

R: How did you feel?

M: Really worried.

R: Why were you worried?

M: Because I was new to the area and I didn't know the school at all.

R: Where did you live before?

M: Leeds, in the north of England.

R: How many people did you already know at the school?

M: One! My next-door neighbour, Ella.

R: Who was the first person you met at school?

M: Jack. He sat next to me in my first lesson.

R: What was your first lesson?

M: Maths. I really enjoyed it because I thought Mr Roach was really funny!

4.3

1 This is my favourite bag. I bought it in Spain and it cost me twenty-five euros.

2 I can't believe this pen is twelve pounds! That's really too expensive!

3 Have you got any money? I need two pounds twenty for my bus ticket.

4 These sunglasses were a bargain! They were only six dollars fifty.

5 How much are these? Are they all eighty cents?

6 You're so lucky! I can't believe your gran gave you fifty pounds!

4.6 and 4.7

1

A: How was your shopping trip, Emma?

B: Good, thanks, Gran. I bought this new notebook. Do you like it?

A: Haven't you got enough notebooks? I thought you got one for your birthday.

B: I did, but this one's for my English homework. Anyway, my other notebook's full of drawings now.

A: Oh, I see. Anyway, come and have lunch now.

2

A: I bought you new trainers for school, Jack.

B: Thanks, Dad! Oh …

A: What's wrong? I thought you liked that shop. Are they the wrong size?

B: Oh no, I am a thirty-seven and that shop has the best trainers! It's just I need black ones. It's the school rules.

A: Oh, I didn't know. No problem, we can change them tomorrow.

3

A: Hi, Adam. It's Sarah.

B: Sorry, I can't hear you very well.

A: It's Sarah! Your sister!

B: Oh hi.

A: I'm just leaving college and I need to buy some milk and bread on the way home for Mum. Can you catch the bus after school and wait for me at the entrance of the supermarket in town?

B: Yeah, OK. See you later.

4

A: Did you see anything for your sister's birthday, Tom?

B: I don't really know what clothes she likes. It's hard shopping for the coolest girl in the school!

A: She likes books. What about the book shop? Or we can go to that gift shop on the high street.

B: You're right, she loves reading. Good idea, let's go there.

5

A: Shall we go shopping now and get your new jacket, Sue?

B: Can we buy it online instead, Mum? I haven't got much time to practise my guitar before the concert.

A: Don't you want to try it on? And the shop in town has a sale.

B: It's the same sale online and I tried the jacket on last Saturday.

A: Alright then.

5.5 and 5.6

1

A: I'm really thirsty! Can we get a drink before we go in and watch the film?

B: Good idea. How much are they? I've only got three pounds left.

A: Me too. Oh, they're three pounds forty. Oh no, that's the large; the small's two pounds ninety. Do you want lemonade or cola?

B: Cola, please!

A: OK, I'll get two colas.

2

A: Hi, Anna. Did you have a good weekend?

B: Yes, thanks. I went to the theatre with my cousin, Jackie. We watched a really funny comedian.

A: That sounds good. Is Jackie your cousin with the long blonde hair and glasses?

B: That's my other cousin. Jackie also wears glasses but has brown hair. You met her at my party.

A: Oh, I remember.

3

A: Aaron, it's a quarter to ten. Are you ready to leave?

B: Why? What's happening?

A: It's the first day of your mum's art exhibition. It starts at half past ten and it takes twenty minutes to get there.

B: Oh, OK, Dad. I'm coming.

A: OK. Well, hurry up – and wear something nice!

4

A: Hi, Barney. How was your first music lesson?

B: Good, thanks, Mum. My teacher's really nice and he's an amazing guitarist!

A: Really? Maybe that's something you can try too?

B: Yeah, I'd like to get better at keyboards first, though. My teacher gave me lots of practice to do. I'm learning to play an Ed Sheeran song.

5

A: Hi, Dad. Where's Katya? I thought she was watching the horror film on TV in the lounge.

B: She was, but she's in her bedroom now. She said it was too noisy down here!

A: Oh, OK. Where's the laptop?

B: Katya took it from the kitchen and took it upstairs with her. She's watching the film on the laptop.

6.5–6.7

M = Melissa   J = Jack

M: Hi, Jack!

J: Oh hi, Melissa.

M: So, are you ready for your party on Saturday?

J: Yes, I think so. My cousin Alex, from France, is coming too. He's going to catch the Saturday morning ferry with his parents.

M: Cool! Do you want me to come round before the party on Saturday – to help get the house ready? I can cycle round after lunch.

J: Yes, please – that will be a big help. I'm going to meet Lily at the bus stop at three. So, she can help us, too.

M: Will Ewan be on the same bus?

J: Actually, he'll be at his uncle's house at the weekend. You know, the uncle with the cool motorbike. He'll come on the underground as his uncle lives right next to a station.

M: Did you invite Henry?

J: Yes, he's catching the train from Glasgow early Saturday morning. I think it's a five-hour journey. It's much quicker by plane, but also too expensive!

M: And Emma? Is she coming?

J: Yes, her brother's driving her to the party on his way to the cinema.

M: Great! I can't wait!

AUDIOSCRIPTS

6.8

A: Where are you going on holiday this summer, Oliver?

B: I'm going to Spain.

A: Lucky you! When are you going?

B: On the twenty-first of July.

A: How are you getting there? Are you flying?

B: No, we're going by boat.

A: Really? That sounds good. How long are you going for?

B: Two weeks. I can't wait!

A: Are you staying in a hotel?

B: No, we're camping – we're staying in a tent.

A: I love camping! Are you going with your family?

B: Just my mum and brother. My dad's working, so he can't come.

7.2

1   The ball in this sport is an unusual shape. It's not round, but oval – like an egg. In this sport two teams try to score points by carrying the ball across a special line or kicking the ball over and between metal posts in the shape of the letter H.

2   In this sport two teams of eleven players try to score points by hitting a small, hard ball with a bat, and running between two sets of small wooden sticks. The players usually wear white shirts and trousers and the sport is very popular in countries like England, India and Pakistan. One game can last days!

3   This sport is really popular in North America. In this game there are two teams of nine players. A player hits a ball with a bat and tries to run around a square on a large field before the other team returns the ball.

4   People sometimes play this sport on the beach. In this game two teams use their hands to hit a large ball backwards and forwards over a high net. The ball can't touch the ground.

5   This is a water sport. In this sport you need a board with a large sail. You stand on the board, hold onto the sail and travel across the top of the water.

6   You play this game outside on grass. Each player has a long thin stick and tries to hit a small ball into nine or eighteen small holes.

7.3–7.5

1

A: Do you want to come surfing this afternoon, Lara?

B: I'm not very good at surfing, Alice. I'm having lessons, but I have to practise more before I go out on my own. How about swimming instead?

A: Yeah, sure. I learned a great diving trick at swimming club.

B: I want to learn to dive! It looks so cool!

A: I can teach you.

2

A: Mum, where's my football shirt? I have to wear it for football practice.

B: Isn't it under your bed, Jess?

A: I just looked there. It was dirty, so maybe it's in the washing machine?

B: I did some washing yesterday. Maybe it's with the clean washing on the kitchen table.

A: It is! Thanks, Mum. I'll put it in my sports bag before I forget!

3

A: Hi, Ann. Do you know what time gymnastics club starts? Is it at three forty-five?

B: Are you going too, Jo? Brilliant! It's three fifteen until four forty-five. Do you want to go together?

A: OK, great. Shall we meet outside the gym at three o'clock?

B: Yeah. See you then.

4

A: Hi, Isaac.

B: Hi, Rob. Did you have a good birthday last week? Did you get those trainers?

A: These? Oh, I got these months ago. I got a new racket. My parents bought it for me.

B: For badminton?

A: Tennis. It's really cool – I'll show you next time we have a game together.

5

A: Hi, Matt. I like your new goggles.

B: Thanks, Kate.

A: Were they expensive? I have to get some new ones. Mine were four pounds ninety-nine, but they broke after the second time I wore them!

B: I got mine online for eight pounds forty-nine, but in the shops they're fourteen pounds ninety-nine. They're really good for diving.

A: I think I'll get some. Can you send me the website later?

8.2 and 8.3

North America

South America

Europe

Africa

Asia

Australia

Antarctica

8.4–8.6

D = Dad   L = Lucy

D: Lucy, dinner's ready in five minutes!

L: OK, Dad. Do you want to look at my geography project?

D: Is this the one about mountains?

L: We did mountains last month and then rainforests. We're learning about rivers and lakes now. Do you like these photos?

D: They're great.

L: I downloaded some interesting photos from the internet, but then I found these in a magazine. I thought they were clearer and the colours were just as good. Have you ever seen any of these lakes or rivers, Dad?

D: I went on a Mississippi river boat when I was a student, but I've never seen the Amazon or the Nile.

L: I'd like to visit Lake Victoria. It's the largest Lake in Africa. It's three hundred and twenty-two kilometres long! It looks amazing!

D: It does.

L: There's a rainy season from March to May. You know it can be cold there, too.

D: Really?

L: Yes. In June the temperature can be fifteen degrees in the day and two degrees at night. That's a difference of over ten degrees!

D: It sounds like you've done a lot of studying about Lake Victoria!

L: Yes, I have. Can we go there on holiday, Dad?

D: It's a great place to visit, but it costs a lot of money. Maybe in the future, when you have a good job, you can save money and go. Anyway, time to eat now!

8.7 and 8.8

1   Have you ever seen a full moon?

2   Has your teacher ever been to Australia?

3   Have your parents ever gone mountain climbing?

4   Has your best friend ever slept in a rainforest?

5   Have you ever found a mouse in your house?

6   Have you ever swum in the sea?

8.9 and 8.10

Z = Zach   E = Ella

Z: It's boiling hot today. Let's go for a swim in the river.

E: I don't know. I think it's dangerous swimming in the river because the water travels so fast.

Z: Yes, you're right. How about we catch the bus to the coast?

E: I'm not sure. The bus costs a lot of money. Why don't we walk to the lake and have a swim?

Z: Because there's a sailing competition there today. We can't swim.

E: Yeah, you're right. I remember now. The woods will be cool because of all the trees.

Z: Great idea. I'll get some food from home and we can have a picnic.

9.1 and 9.2

A = Alex   D = Dad

A: Dad, will you let me have a party if I do well in my school exams?

D: A party? I'm not sure, Alex. I don't want lots of people in the house.

A: If I have a party, we'll stay in the garden. We can have a barbecue.

D: Well, that's different then. But not too many friends. I don't want the whole school here!

A: No, Dad, I'll only invite about ten friends.

D: And how much will a party cost me?

A: Well, if everyone brings some food, it won't cost much at all. Please, Dad! I've worked really hard.

D: OK, I don't mind. But you'll have to ask your mum first.

9.3

A

A: Wow! That's a big breakfast.

B: I know! If I don't have a good breakfast, I'm really hungry by ten o'clock. What do you have?

A: I usually eat fresh fruit for breakfast.

B

A: I feel really tired and I'm bored.

B: Why don't you get some fresh air? Go on your bike for a bit. If you do some exercise, you'll feel better.

C

A: Do you want to go for a walk? It's really sunny outside.

B: That sounds great, but I've got so much homework to do.

A: You need to find time to relax, too. A short walk will help you study better. Come on!

9.6–9.8

Hi, Carla. It's Lisa. I'm phoning to let you know about the school picnic. You know it was on Sunday? Well, they've changed it because of the weather. It's now tomorrow, Saturday. We're going to have the picnic in the park on Grove Road. That's G–R–O–V–E. We plan to have the picnic around half past one, but you should get to the park at one to help get things ready. I'm leaving my house at half past twelve, so maybe we can walk together? It doesn't cost anything, but everyone has to bring some food. The teacher gave us a list. I'm bringing salad and the teacher wants you to bring some fruit. Ella's baking one of her amazing cakes! Oh, and you should wear trainers as we'll play some games in the park. If you have any other questions, you can call Mrs Sharp. She's organising the picnic. Her number is 0788 534 566. Anyway, I'm pleased you're feeling better now. We missed you at school. I can't wait to see you tomorrow!

9.10 and 9.11

E = Examiner   L = Lucas   R = Rosa

E: You are going to talk together. Here are some pictures that show everyday activities. Do you like these everyday activities? Say why or why not. I'll say that again. Do you like these everyday activities? Say why or why not. All right? Now, talk together.

L: Well, I enjoy reading because it helps me relax. What about you, Rosa? Do you like reading?

R: Yes, I do, but I don't read that much in my free time. I enjoy doing exercise. I often go to the gym with my friends and we do different exercise classes.

L: I don't really like the gym because I don't like doing exercise indoors. I prefer being outdoors and going for a walk or run in the woods near my house. Do you like spending time outdoors, too?

R: Yes, I love being outdoors because the fresh air makes me feel good. I also like spending free time at home. I love cooking for my friends. Do you like cooking at home?

L: Not really, because I'm not very good at cooking. I enjoy playing music at home. I play the guitar and I have to practise a lot because I'm in a band.

E: So, Lucas, which of these activities do you like best?

L: Well, I like playing my guitar best because music is very important to me.

E: And, Rosa, which of these activities do you like best?

R: My favourite activity is baking because I love making food for my friends and family.

10.1

1

A: Hi, Lucy. Did you hear that Miss Parker's leaving?

B: I know, and she's my favourite teacher. I'm going to buy her a leaving present.

A: What are you going to get?

B: I thought about flowers, but they don't last long. I'm going to get her a plant. I thought about a vase, but they're too expensive.

A: I'm sure she'll love it!

2

A: Are you going to judo club today?

B: Yes, I am. I'll see you there at four.

A: It's later today. There's a badminton competition in the sports hall until quarter past four and so we're starting half an hour later, at a quarter to five. The judo teacher sent everyone a message about it.

B: Oh, I probably forgot. Thanks for letting me know!

3

A: I like this photo, Tom. Is the girl in the striped T-shirt your sister?

B: That's my cousin; my sister's standing next to her.

A: But I thought your sister was at primary school.

B: That's my little brother. My sister's at university. She's wearing my cap in the photo. She always borrows my stuff – and usually without asking!

A: My sister's the same!

4

A: Hi, Nick. Did you have fun surfing yesterday?

B: We didn't go because it was really windy, which is good for surfing, but not for beginners like us!

A: That's a shame.

B: It was fine. We left the beach and went to the woods. We went mountain biking. It rained a bit but we didn't get very wet. It's really sunny today.

5

A: Are you going on the school trip to the Science Museum?

B: Yes, I am. I've got the money to pay Mr Jones today. It's twelve pounds fifty, isn't it?

A: I thought it only cost six pounds fifty to get into the museum.

B: You're right, it does. But we also have to pay for the coach, so that's another six pounds.

A: Oh, I see.

10.2

Hello, everyone. As you know, we're going on our theatre trip next week. As well as myself, Mr Harrison and Mr Roach will come. The theatre we're visiting is called the Adelphi Theatre. That's spelled A–D–E–L–P–H–I. Find out about it on the internet. We wanted to go on the twenty-fifth of March, but because of the basketball competition we've moved it to the twenty-fourth of March. We'll meet outside the school gym. You'll need to be at school before lessons start at nine o'clock. We'll meet at a quarter past eight and we'll go at half past eight. Please get to school early – if you're late, you'll miss the coach. So, make sure you catch the earlier bus or train to school that day. The theatre is about an hour and a half from school. You will need to bring your own lunch – something healthy, please. And you will all have to leave your phones at home – I won't be happy if I see any on the day! Any questions?

10.3

A: Hi, Isobel. I didn't see you after school yesterday.

B: Oh hi, Finlay. No, I was at that new art class.

A: Oh I heard about that. Mr Hill teaches the class, doesn't he? He's a friend of the art teacher at school. Mr Hill's a really good artist. He lives in our town – next to Mark's parents' house.

B: That's right. He's really nice.

A: So, what did you do in the class yesterday?

B: Well, we looked at lots of photos of different artists' work. And then we did some drawings. We'll do painting next week.

A: I'd like to do something like that, but isn't it expensive to buy all that art equipment?

B: You don't have to. They give you what you need. You just need to bring a large folder to put all your artwork in. They even have old shirts to wear.

A: Maybe I'll ask if I can go next week.

B: I think you'll like it. Art lessons at school can be a bit boring, but this is different. In fact, I felt the time went too quickly. It's not too easy and not too difficult.

A: What are you painting next week?

B: We're going to do paintings of each other.

A: I'm afraid I'll do terrible paintings of people and they'll be upset. I'm not very good!

B: You'll be fine!

10.4

16

Hi, Rosie, it's Mum here. On your way home, can you get some flour, please? I want to make your aunty a birthday cake. I won't make it until this evening, so you don't need to come home early. I hope you're having fun at your friend's. I'm going to collect your sister from athletics club now. See you later.

17

A: I loved going for a swim in the sea today.

B: Me too! I think the best part of the day was when we played volleyball.

A: I agree. And then those delicious ice creams from the beach café!

B: You mean the ones you dropped on the floor? You need to buy me another ice cream tomorrow!

18

Before you go, don't forget about your homework. You need to write a story about a frightening experience. It's not necessary for the story to be true, but it does need to be interesting! I don't mind about the length. Some very good stories can be fairly short, but it does need a clear beginning, middle and end. So, please …

19

A: Hi, Martha. You missed a great party on Saturday. Ella said you had stomach ache.

B: I heard it was a good party. It wasn't my stomach; I had a temperature. I was really annoyed I missed it.

A: Are you feeling better now?

B: I felt better by Sunday morning, but now I've got toothache! I'm going to the dentist's later.

20

A: Hi, Liam. Did you have a good holiday?

B: Absolutely brilliant, thanks. I've been windsurfing in lots of places, but this was the best. It was an amazing lake.

A: Did you try sailing?

B: I wanted to but we ran out of time. I went fishing one day, though. And I caught a fish! Not bad for a complete beginner!

A: Great!

10.5

A: So how was your school trip, Alice?

B: Great, thanks, Grandad. We did lots of activities. We arrived on Sunday, we had dinner and then played table tennis until it was time for bed.

A: And what about Monday?

B: The plan was to go climbing in the mountains, but the weather was terrible, so we did indoor activities. I played badminton and some others played basketball.

A: Did the weather improve?

B: Oh yes, we went to the beach on Tuesday. We rode horses there! It was so much fun!

A: It sounds it! Did you go swimming at the beach?

B: Some people went swimming on Wednesday. I forgot to pack a swimsuit, unfortunately. I joined the group that learned to sail instead.

A: That sounds even more fun!

B: It was. On Thursday one group went horse-riding and the other group, which I was in, went on a bike ride. And then it was Friday, the last day – and we finally climbed the mountain. It was great, but it was more tiring than cycling! Do you want to see my photos?

A: Of course!

10.6

What's your name?

How old are you?

Where do you come from?

Where do you live?

Thank you.

10.7

Now let's talk about holidays. Where do you like going on holiday?

How often do you go on holiday?

Now, please tell me something about your best holiday.

10.8

Now you are going to talk together. Here are some pictures that show different free time activities.

Do you like these free time activities? Say why or why not.

I'll say that again. Do you like these free time activities? Say why or why not.

All right? Now talk together.

10.9

Do you think painting is easy? Why or why not?

Do you think cycling with friends is fun? Why or why not?

Do you think playing board games is boring? Why or why not?

So, which of these free time activities do you like best?

Thank you.

10.10

Do you prefer to spend your free time with friends or alone? Why?

What would you like to do in your free time next weekend? Why?

Thank you. That is the end of the test.

IRREGULAR VERB LIST

Verb	Past simple	Past participle
be	was/were	been
become	became	become
begin	began	begun
bring	brought	brought
build	built	built
buy	bought	bought
catch	caught	caught
choose	chose	chosen
come	came	come
cost	cost	cost
cut	cut	cut
do	did	done
draw	drew	drawn
drink	drank	drunk
drive	drove	driven
eat	ate	eaten
fall	fell	fallen
feed	fed	fed
feel	felt	felt
fight	fought	fought
find	found	found
fly	flew	flown
forget	forgot	forgotten
get	got	got
give	gave	given
go	went	gone/been
have	had	had
hear	heard	heard
keep	kept	kept
know	knew	known
learn	learnt/learned	learnt/learned
leave	left	left
let	let	let

Verb	Past simple	Past participle
lose	lost	lost
make	made	made
mean	meant	meant
meet	met	met
pay	paid	paid
put	put	put
read	read	read
ride	rode	ridden
ring	rang	rung
run	ran	run
say	said	said
see	saw	seen
sell	sold	sold
send	sent	sent
show	showed	shown
shut	shut	shut
sit	sat	sat
sleep	slept	slept
speak	spoke	spoken
spend	spent	spent
stand	stood	stood
steal	stole	stolen
swim	swam	swum
take	took	taken
teach	taught	taught
tell	told	told
think	thought	thought
understand	understood	understood
wake	woke	woken
wear	wore	worn
win	won	won
write	wrote	written

EXAM OVERVIEW

Cambridge English Qualification A2 Key for Schools Exam, otherwise known as *Cambridge Key for Schools*, is an examination set at A2 level of the Common European Framework of Reference for Languages (CEFR). It is made up of **three papers**, each testing a different area of ability in English: Reading and Writing, Listening, and Speaking.

Reading and Writing	1 hour	50% of the marks
Listening	35 minutes (approximately)	25% of the marks
Speaking	8–10 minutes for each pair of students (approximately)	25% of the marks

All the examination questions are task-based. Rubrics (instructions) are important and candidates should read them carefully. They set the context and give important information about the tasks. There are separate answer sheets for recording answers for the Reading and Writing paper and the Listening paper.

Paper	Format	Task focus
Reading and Writing Seven Parts 32 questions	**Part 1:** three-option multiple choice. Reading six short texts and choosing the correct answer	**Part 1:** reading short texts for the main idea, detail, and writer's purpose.
	Part 2: matching. Reading three short texts or paragraphs on the same topic and matching the correct text or paragraph to the question.	**Part 2:** reading for detailed understanding.
	Part 3: three-option multiple choice. Five multiple-choice questions.	**Part 3:** reading for main idea(s), detail, opinion, attitude and writer's purpose.
	Part 4: three-option multiple-choice cloze. Reading a text with six gaps and selecting the correct word to complete each gap.	**Part 4:** reading and identifying appropriate word.
	Part 5: open cloze. Short text with six gaps. Completing the text with one word in each gap.	**Part 5:** reading and writing appropriate word to fill in the gap.
	Part 6: guided writing; writing a short message. Reading an email or reading about a situation and writing an email.	**Part 6:** Writing an email to a friend including three pieces of information. 25 words or more.
	Part 7: guided writing; writing a short narrative. Three pictures which show a story.	**Part 7:** Writing the short story shown in the three pictures. 35 words or more.
Listening Five Parts 25 questions	**Part 1:** three-option multiple choice. Listening to five short dialogues and choosing the correct picture for each answer.	**Part 1:** listening to identify key information.
	Part 2: gap fill. Listening to a longer monologue and writing the missing word, number, date or time in five gaps.	**Part 2:** listening and writing down information.
	Part 3: three-option multiple choice. Listening to a longer dialogue and choosing the correct answer to five questions.	**Part 3:** listening to identify key information, feelings and opinions.
	Part 4: three-option multiple choice. Listening to five short dialogues or monologues and choosing the correct answer for each text-based question.	**Part 4:** listening for gist, main idea or topic.
	Part 5: matching. Listening to a longer dialogue and matching five questions with seven options. An example is given.	**Part 5:** listening to identify specific information.
Speaking Two Parts	**Part 1:** interview: examiner-led conversation. 3-4 minutes	**Part 1:** giving personal information.
	Part 2: collaborative task: two-way conversation with visual prompt. Examiner asks two more questions to broaden the topic. 5-6 minutes	**Part 2:** asking and answering simple questions, expressing likes and dislikes and giving reasons.